The Anthropology of Florida

CLASSICS IN SOUTHEASTERN ARCHAEOLOGY
Stephen Williams, *Series Editor*

The Anthropology of Florida

Aleš Hrdlička

THE UNIVERSITY OF ALABAMA PRESS
Tuscaloosa

Dedicated to the memory of Professor Frederic W. Putnam

The University of Alabama Press
Tuscaloosa, Alabama 35487-0380

Published by The University of Alabama Press, 2007

∞
The paper on which this book is printed meets the minimum requirements of American National Standard for Information Science—Permanence of Paper for Printed Library Materials, ANSI Z39.48-1984.

Library of Congress Cataloging-in-Publication Data

Hrdlička, Aleš, 1869–1943.
  The anthropology of Florida / Ales Hrdlicka.
    p. cm. — (Classics in southeastern archaeology)
  Includes index.
  Originally published: Deland, Fla. : Florida State Historical Society, 1922, in series: Publications of the Florida State Historical Society ; no. 1.
  ISBN-13: 978-0-8173-5359-9 (pbk. : alk. paper)
  ISBN-10: 0-8173-5359-3
  1. Indians of North America—Florida—Antiquities. 2. Seminole Indians—Antiquities. 3. Florida—Antiquities. I. Title. II. Series.
  E78.F6H73 2006
  975.9'01—dc22
                        2006009146

INTRODUCTION TO THE NEW EDITION
ALEŠ HRDLIČKA'S 1918 SURVEY OF SOUTHWEST FLORIDA

Aleš Hrdlička (1869–1943) (figure 1) is generally regarded as the father of American physical anthropology or bioanthropology, the biological study of humans and primates. An indefatigable researcher, writer, and collector, he made monumental impacts on the field. Not only was he largely responsible for amassing and cataloguing the substantial collections of human skeletal remains in the U.S. National Museum (now the National Museum of Natural History, Smithsonian Institution), but he was also the founder of the *American Journal of Physical Anthropology* and was its editor from 1918 until 1942 (Spencer 1979: chs. 12–13; Stewart 1940). In addition, he was the founder (in 1929) and first president (1930–1932) of the American Association of Physical Anthropologists (Stewart 1940:19).

In the midst of his remarkable career, Hrdlička spent four weeks conducting field research in southwest Florida, and the results of this work were published in 1922 as *The Anthropology of Florida*. The circumstances that led to his trip and the difficulties he encountered are in themselves a compelling story. To fully appreciate his contributions to Florida anthropology, however, including those contained in this volume, it is important to understand him as a person and to examine both published works and unpublished documents that provide background to his 1918 fieldwork and the resulting publication.

Figure 1. Aleš Hrdlička on April 23, 1942. Courtesy of The Wistar Institute, Wistar Archive Collections, Philadelphia, Pennsylvania.

Aleš Hrdlička: A Brief Biography

Biographical information about Aleš Hrdlička is available from several sources. A succinct overview of his accomplishments and a list of his publications through 1939 were provided by T. Dale Stewart (1940) in a paper prepared as part of a tribute to Hrdlička on the occasion of his seventieth birthday. A short professional obituary was published by M. F. Ashley Montagu (1944). Adolph H. Schultz (1944) wrote a biographical overview on behalf of the National Academy of Sciences. A brief biography from the Czech perspective was written by M. Prokopec (1991). A useful chronology of his life was provided by Robert L. Montgomery (1996:3–6). The most exhaustive biography, however, was a two-volume doctoral dissertation by Frank Spencer (1979). These sources contain conflicting information and errors, especially about his early life. Spencer's in-depth biography is considered the most reliable source due to its comprehensive nature and inclusion of information obtained from relatives of Hrdlička.

Born on March 29, 1869, in Humpolec, Bohemia (which later became part of Czechoslovakia), Hrdlička emigrated with his father to America at the age of twelve (Schultz 1944:305; Spencer 1979:30). They arrived in New York City in September of 1881 (Spencer 1979:19, 30). His mother and six siblings followed in 1882, and the family settled in New York City. He earned a degree in medicine from the Eclectic Medical College of the City of New York in 1892 (Spencer 1979:44). In 1893, wanting to broaden his medical knowledge, he enrolled at the New York Homeopathic Medical College, graduating with a degree in homeopathic medicine in the spring of 1894 (Prokopec 1991:311; Spencer 1979:50–51).

During the 1890s, Hrdlička worked at several hospitals in New York City and developed a great interest in human anatomy and variation among populations. Also during this decade, the Eclectic Medical College hired him to teach medical diagnosis and anatomy to medical students at the Margaret Strachan Home for Wayward Girls (Spencer 1979:44–46). In 1891, he met a prospective medical student named Marie Strickler. Hrdlička and this Frenchwoman struck up a friendship that grew into a romantic relationship over the next few years. They were married on August 6, 1896 (Spencer 1979:ch. 2). After her death in 1918, he married Vilemina Mansfield (Montgomery 1996:5; Spencer 1979:71–73).

In the late 1890s, Hrdlička met Professor Frederic Ward Putnam, who was both Curator of the Peabody Museum of Archaeology and Ethnology at Harvard University from 1874 to 1909 and Curator (and founder) of the Department of Anthropology at the American Museum of Natural History in New York from 1894 to 1903 (Phillips 1973:ix). Through his acquaintance with Putnam, Hrdlička arranged to accompany Carl Lumholtz on an American Museum of Natural History archaeological expedition to Mexico in 1898, where he was able to record medical and physical anthropological information about the Tarahumares, Huichols, Tepehuanes, and other Indian groups living in the region (Lumholtz and Hrdlička 1898). Over the next several years, he participated in a number of the Museum's expeditions to the southwestern United States and northern Mexico, during which he studied both excavated skeletons and living Indian populations (Anonymous 1902; Hrdlička 1901, 1902, 1903, 1908; Stewart 1940:10–11).

Hrdlička's studies eventually brought him into contact with anthropologists at the Smithsonian Institution and the Army Medical Museum in Washington, D.C. He developed a strong friendship with William H. Holmes, who had been appointed the second director of the Smithsonian's Bureau of American Ethnology when the first director, Major John Wesley Powell, died in 1902 (Judd 1967:21–23). In

1903, largely through Holmes's influence, Hrdlička was hired to create a Division of Physical Anthropology in the U.S. National Museum at the Smithsonian Institution, and he remained with the Smithsonian for the rest of his career (Judd 1967:69–70; Meltzer 1994:13; Stewart 1940:11–12). He interacted frequently with Holmes and authored six publications in the Bureau of American Ethnology's Bulletin series (Hrdlička 1907, 1908, 1909, 1912, 1916, 1918b; Judd 1967:70; Meltzer and Dunnell 1992:xxii–xxiii).

Both Hrdlička and Holmes were convinced that there were no geologically ancient (pre-*Homo sapiens sapiens,* such as Neanderthals) humans in the New World (Holmes 1918, 1925; Hrdlička 1907). While subsequent research has demonstrated that this is indeed correct, Hrdlička was also adamant that no humans were in the New World during the Pleistocene Epoch. He devoted a great deal of time and energy to studying skeletal remains of purported late Pleistocene age and arguing that they dated to more recent times (Hrdlička 1907, 1918b; Meltzer 1994:14–15). His strong bias in this regard and his major stature in the field hindered debate on the matter for many years (Wilmsen 1965:179), although it is true that most of the cases he studied did indeed date from more recent times.

The Folsom Paleoindian discoveries in 1927 softened Hrdlička's stance somewhat (Meltzer 1994:15–17), but he was stubborn and certain in his belief that he was right. As one of his biographers stated: "Thus, once having become convinced that man's arrival in America was of comparatively recent date, he steadfastly clung to and passionately fought for this conclusion to the end of his life, even in view of evidence demanding a reconsideration of the problem of the antiquity of man in the New World" (Schultz 1944:312–313).

In addition to his strong opinions about peopling of the New World, Hrdlička was well-known for other eccentricities. He did not believe that women should be involved in science, and would reportedly avoid interacting with them at meetings (Montagu 1944:116; but cf. Montgomery 1996:2). He was quite averse to statistical analyses in physical anthropology (Montagu 1944:115; Montgomery 1996:2). He was also very frugal and lived an exceptionally austere lifestyle (Schultz 1944:314; Spencer 1979:754). Although he projected a serious mien, especially in photographs, those who knew him well wrote that he was actually a very kind and generous man with a naive or shy side (Montagu 1944:116; Schultz 1944:315).

During his career Hrdlička traveled extensively, conducting research on every continent except Antarctica (Montgomery 1996). A tireless worker, he amassed an amazing amount of data and published extensively (Stewart 1940; Spencer 1979). Despite his eccentricities and often unpopular opinions, he interacted widely with colleagues and was a well-respected scientist. By the time of his death on September 6, 1943, he was one of the most renowned physical anthropologists in the world.

Florida Connections

Prior to Hrdlička's 1918 expedition to Florida, he had traveled to that state several times (Hrdlička 1922:foreword) and he was also a central participant in debates about supposed early remains recovered there. His first trip to Florida was in February, 1906, when he visited the town of Osprey south of Sarasota (Stewart 1940:12). At the time, he was in the process of completing one of his books, *Skeletal Remains Suggesting or Attributed to Early Man in North America* (Hrdlička 1907). In the course of compiling information on skeletal discoveries in Florida, he conducted chemical and physical analyses of fossilized human remains recovered from the Osprey area in the 1870s and 1880s (1907:53–60). Not surprisingly, he had concluded "that there is absolutely nothing in these bones which would suggest great or even considerable antiquity, geologically speaking" (Hrdlička 1907:59).

Because of the fossilized condition of the bones, he believed it would be wise to visit the area (1907:60). He was accompanied by T. Wayland Vaughan, a geologist from the U.S. Geological Survey. For two weeks, they revisited and investigated some of the sites, and reached the conclusion that all of the remains were of a geologically recent age (Hrdlička 1907:60–66). Geological and archaeological data from the area clearly indicated that the remains were only a few centuries old.

It was Hrdlička's interest in early human remains that led to an invitation from Elias H. Sellards to visit Florida a decade later in October, 1916. Educated at the University of Kansas and Yale University, Sellards was the first State Geologist of Florida. At that time, there were no professional archaeologists based at universities in the state, nor were there any museums or state agencies employing archaeologists, so Sellards and his staff engaged in archaeological studies in addition to carrying out geological and natural history research (Lane 1998:11, 16–17).

Sellards had been investigating a locality at Vero that yielded human bones in association with bones of animals that had been extinct since the Pleistocene (Sellards 1916a, 1916b, 1917a, 1917b). He was convinced of the antiquity of the human remains, and invited Hrdlička and a number of other scientists from many disciplines to visit the site and see for themselves the strata and to conduct any investigations they wished. Hrdlička (1917a) therefore traveled to Vero and had workmen expose a large cut along the canal bank where the remains had been found. The findings of the various scientists were conflicting as to their age, and controversy ensued, with Hrdlička and William H. Holmes leading the anti-Pleistocene camp (Meltzer 1991:24). Hrdlička was probably right in this case, although there is still uncertainty (Milanich 1994:8).

Upon leaving Vero, Hrdlička traveled across the state to Fort Myers, where he did a quick investigation of a site on Demere or Demorey

Key. As at Osprey, he showed that human bones embedded in coquina-like rock were from recent times, not Pleistocene or older (Hrdlička 1917b).

Spencer (1979:754, n. 2) reported that Hrdlička apparently purchased a "cottage" somewhere in Florida for his wife in 1915. He sold this house after her death in 1918, and bought 10 acres of land in Moore Haven, Florida. This property was sold at a profit six years later.

His 1918 field trip (the basis for this volume) was his longest excursion into Florida. The project was probably influential in his later decision to actively support the establishment of Everglades National Park (Hrdlička 1932). In succeeding years, Hrdlička continued to voice his opinions about skeletal remains found in the state. His reaction (Hrdlička 1937:95–98) to the supposedly Pleistocene finds at Melbourne (Gidley and Loomis 1926; Loomis 1924, 1925, 1926) was predictable.

The Anthropology of Florida

Hrdlička's first wife, Marie Strickler Hrdlička, died on October 18, 1918, after several years of poor health, probably due to complications from diabetes (Spencer 1979:63–64). Aleš Hrdlička was devoted to his wife, and her loss after 22 years of marriage devastated him. He was consumed by grief that lasted for weeks and led to such a state of mental and physical exhaustion that he began having heart palpitations and difficulty sleeping. He therefore traveled to the Battle Creek Sanitarium in Michigan for a medical examination, but they could find no physical problems and diagnosed him with exhaustion.

The doctor recommended that he take time off from his work to rest (Spencer 1979:70–71). William H. Holmes and J. Walter Fewkes of the Bureau of American Ethnology agreed, and they came up with funds for Hrdlička to take a brief trip in November, 1918, for convalescence, although some research would have to be carried out in order to justify use of government funds (and knowing Hrdlička's work ethic, it would be hard to imagine him just relaxing for two weeks) (Hrdlička 1922: Foreword).

His primary aim on the project was to locate archaeological sites in southwest Florida from Fort Myers through the Ten Thousand Islands and inland to the Lake Okeechobee basin, and he was also hoping to measure and collect human skeletal remains from some of them. In addition, Hrdlička wanted to contact some Seminoles to record anthropological data (Hrdlička 1922:14).

He spent four weeks on the project, and quickly came face to face with the realities of conducting archaeological work in the region. He expected to encounter troublesome insects, but the unbelievable hordes of mosquitoes were overwhelming. His field notes (Hrdlička 1918a) make frequent mention of them, along with chiggers. Due to the great numbers of insects and the sparse human population of the area, he was unable to find people to employ as field crews, so he failed to carry out any excavations or to collect any new bone specimens. Fortunately, he was able to hire a local guide, because the few available maps of the rivers and keys were sorely inadequate.

His schedule was as follows: Leaving Washington on October 30, 1918, he arrived in Fort Myers on November 3 and spent the next month traveling the area and making notes on the sites that he learned of from local people. He visited and took notes on at least 77 sites during this time (Hrdlička 1918a). Some of these were ones he had read about in Clarence B. Moore's (1900, 1905, 1907) publications, but many were previously unrecorded. He did an admirable job of recording measurements and topographic details, even though clouds of mosquitoes necessitated brief visits at times. He also recorded information on artifacts, burials, or other features collected or encountered by local residents.

Hrdlička's (1918a) field notes offer an interesting glimpse of the residents of southwest Florida in 1918. Most of them were impoverished and lived in isolated areas. On more than one occasion, he mentioned that the people were very happy to see him, and were starved for conversation. Most were friendly and generous, providing accommodations in their homes. It would indeed be interesting to know what those people thought of the short, rather stern-looking doctor with a thick Czechoslovakian accent. During that time, influenza was ravaging the country, and Hrdlička noted that several families had members who were seriously ill. Reflecting his medical training, he recorded a few symptoms in his notebook, but there is no indication that he tried to treat any of the sick.

In recording archaeological sites, Hrdlička came prepared to document them with a camera. He soon realized that the thick vegetation generally made this impossible, however. He included a few photographs of sites in the book, such as one of the overgrown sand mound on Horr's Island known as the Blue Hills. For most of the larger sites, he drew rough sketch maps in his notebook (1918a), and published a drawing of the extensive shell mounds and middens at Brown's Place on the Turner River.

Hrdlička's attempts to study living Seminoles were almost totally unsuccessful. He met only four Seminole men the entire time, and was only able to convince one to let him take anthropometric measurements (1922:53–54). This was a 19 or 20 year old man named Boy Jim; he was probably one of the men shown in Plate VII.

When he returned to the Smithsonian in December, 1918, Hrdlička began thinking about how he should report the results of his project. He first published a brief (four pages) illustrated summary of his expedition a few months later (Hrdlička 1919). He was disappointed that he had been unable to collect additional skeletal material and had only gotten measurements on one Seminole. He then decided that he would summarize all the information from previous research on Florida archaeology, physical anthropology, and aboriginal history, and combine this with his own analysis of every human bone from Florida he could find in collections. This information, along with the archaeological data he had gathered, would then compose the most complete summary of anthropological information on Florida. This became *The Anthropology of Florida* (1922).

Hrdlička originally intended to publish the book as part of the *Bulletin* series of the Bureau of American Ethnology. There were apparently several other manuscripts scheduled to be published in the series, causing a substantial delay. In 1921, John B. Stetson, Jr., was visiting the Smithsonian Institution, and in a chance meeting with Hrdlička he learned of the manuscript's existence and the author's concern about the delay. Stetson expressed interest in publishing it, and Hrdlička agreed to turn the manuscript over to the Florida State Historical Society (Hrdlička 1922:Preface; Shofner 2004:28).

John B. Stetson, Jr., was a wealthy student of Florida history who founded the Florida State Historical Society in 1921. This organization was created despite the existence of the Florida Historical Society, which had been founded in 1856. Stetson's aim was to found a society that would pursue an active publication program (Shofner 2004:25–28). By sheer luck, Hrdlička's *The Anthropology of Florida* (1922) became the first publication of Stetson's fledgling society. The Florida State Historical Society published 11 volumes before the stock market crash of 1929. Stetson then lost much of his wealth and was unable to continue his heavy support of the Florida State Historical Society. It became dormant, eventually merging with the Florida Historical Society (Shofner 2004).

Distribution of the book was not as wide as it could have been, and had Hrdlička been aware of Stetson's method of distribution he might have chosen to wait for the book to be published by the Smithsonian

Institution. Stetson (1923) devised a system where the publications of the society would *only* be available to sustaining members, who agreed to purchase all publications put out by the Society. This therefore meant that there were no extra copies for review, exchange, or sale to the general public. Probably as a result of this policy, Stetson lost about $1,000.00 on the book (Shofner 2004:38–39). The rarity of the book is no doubt due to Stetson's very peculiar distribution policy.

The first 52 pages of *The Anthropology of Florida* are devoted to description of the archaeological sites he recorded. Most of these had been visited and/or investigated previously by Frank Hamilton Cushing (Kolianos and Weisman 2005a, 2005b) or Clarence B. Moore (Mitchem 1999), but some were previously unrecorded and Hrdlička's descriptions were the first information available for these sites.

Although the field portion of the research project did not yield the results he would have desired, Hrdlička nevertheless made some enduring contributions to the archaeology of southwest Florida. It should be pointed out that he was only the second researcher to view the archaeology of the region from the anthropological perspective. Like Frank Hamilton Cushing before him (Kolianos and Weisman 2005a, 2005b), he interpreted the sites in terms of populations and activities of people, rather than the antiquarian focus on artifacts typified by Clarence B. Moore and others.

On pages 48–51, Hrdlička (1922) presents his "General Impressions," which in effect are his conclusions from the project. It is worth summarizing these here to highlight the value of this volume. He was the first to publish a classification of site types in the region (Hrdlička1922:48). Although Cushing (Kolianos and Weisman 2005b) was certainly thinking along the same lines, his untimely death in 1900 meant that his manuscript on his Florida research was incomplete and remained unpublished until 2005.

Hrdlička (1922:48–49) also noted the intentional patterning of the large sites and systematic plans of construction. In addition, he recognized that not all shell mounds were middens, but many were intentionally built to aid in protection from storms and tides. He was not the first to make these observations, as Cushing (1896:66–87) had also mentioned them in his Key Marco report, although in a less direct manner.

Like others before him, Hrdlička (1922:48–49) discussed the constructed canals in the region that were obviously associated with the planned archaeological sites. But he went a step further, and pointed out that the canals, associated artificial harbors, and carefully planned shell constructions were a local response to environmental conditions rather than diffusion of ideas from other areas (1922:49).

One of Hrdlička's important observations was that the sites in southwest Florida all have cultural connections with the Charlotte Harbor area. From this he correctly inferred that the people who built and inhabited the shell heaps and other sites were the Calusas (Hrdlička 1922:50). Hrdlička was the first to realize this fact, which has been conclusively demonstrated by subsequent archaeological and ethnohistorical research (Marquardt 1992; Widmer 1988).

In one important respect, however, Hrdlička was mistaken. He believed that the Calusas practiced agriculture (Hrdlička 1922:48–49). This was understandable, since he encountered farmers while traveling about the area, but more recent archaeologists have shown that the Calusas were nonagricultural (Milanich 1994:317).

Because he was unable to carry out in-depth investigations, the archaeological information provided in this volume is best suited to be used as supplementary data. It should be noted, however, that Hrdlička's field notes (1918a) at the National Anthropological Archives contain rough sketches and maps of many of the sites that would be of interest to anyone carrying out archaeological research in the region.

The rest of this book contains an overview of what was known at the time about the Indian tribes of Florida, as well as a comprehensive study of human osteological assemblages from the state. On pages 65–68, Hrdlička (1922) provides the first systematic population estimate for Florida at the time of European contact. He based this on techniques that are still used by many researchers today, namely using the number of sites and the estimated amount of labor required to build them. His estimate (1922:68) of 25,000 to 30,000 would probably be about right for southwest Florida alone, but his discussion indicates that he was referring to the area encompassed by the entire state. Accurately estimating past population sizes is difficult, if not impossible, and even modern researchers cannot agree on Florida's population at the time of initial contact (Dobyns 1983; Hann 1990; Milanich 1987).

Because Hrdlička failed to collect any human bones during his fieldwork, he instead made a monumental effort to study all the collections of Florida human skeletal material in museums and other institutions. This included material excavated by Clarence B. Moore, Jeffries Wyman, and several other researchers, housed in the U.S. National Museum, the Academy of Natural Sciences of Philadelphia, the Wistar Institute of Anatomy and Biology, and other repositories (Hrdlička 1922:81). Concentrating on skull measurements, which was the practice at the time, Hrdlička was able to study 173 crania from all parts of Florida. He then presented the data in tables and made observations about the general physical types of prehistoric Florida Indians and how they compared to native peoples of surrounding regions.

While the skeletal measurements are not exciting reading for most of us, it is important to point out that this was the first comprehensive study of human skeletal remains from Florida. All of Hrdlička's measurements were standardized, so they are still useful for anyone carrying out craniometric research. This segment of the book is part of a larger long-term study of crania and other skeletal remains (Hrdlička 1940), which covered not only remains from Florida but from the entire Southeast. The measurements comprise a set of baseline data that has been used by later researchers, and Hrdlička's careful measurements have been of use to subsequent physical anthropologists carrying out statistical analyses. For instance, Eugene Giles and Orville Elliot (1962) used Hrdlička's data to develop discriminant function formulas for distinguishing distinct populations from cranial measurements.

There is one error in this book that, although minor, should be pointed out. In the first sentence of the last paragraph on page 36, "southeast" should be "northeast." It should also be mentioned that this edition does not include the red and blue shading that was in Plate IX in the original 1922 edition. As the shaded portions were only rough approximations based on preliminary data, this omission should not cause any great difficulty to researchers.

Although this book had its beginning in the tragic death of Marie Hrdlička, its contents are still relevant to Florida anthropologists. This volume will introduce Hrdlička's research to a new generation of scholars.

Acknowledgments

Many people have contributed to the success of this project. Jeannie Sklar and other personnel at the National Anthropological Archives provided access to Hrdlička's field notes, correspondence, and other papers. Carol J. Armstrong facilitated access to the Florida Geological Survey's archives. Personnel of the Florida Master Site File gave me access to Florida archaeological site records. Nina P. Long of The Wistar Institute provided a print and arranged permission for use of the photograph of Hrdlička in this introduction. Executive Director Dr. Lewis N. Wynne and Archivist Debra T. Wynne of the Florida Historical Society kindly provided an original copy of *The Anthropology of Florida* from their library for use in producing this edition. Jerald T. Milanich of the Florida Museum of Natural History and Dale L. Hutchinson of the University of North Carolina aided in obtaining background material. Stephen Williams and an anonymous reviewer read an earlier draft of this introduction and provided detailed comments and suggestions that strengthened it immeasurably. Special thanks go to The University of Alabama Press for seeing this project through to completion.

—Jeffrey M. Mitchem

References Cited

Anonymous

1902   Anthropological Work in the Southwestern United States and Mexico. *American Museum Journal* 2:68–72. American Museum of Natural History, New York.

Cushing, Frank Hamilton

1896   The Pepper-Hearst Expedition: A Preliminary Report on the Exploration of Ancient Key-Dweller Remains on the Gulf Coast of Florida. *Proceedings of the American Philosophical Society* 35(153).

Dobyns, Henry F.

1983   *Their Number Become Thinned: Native Population Dynamics in Eastern North America.* University of Tennessee Press, Knoxville.

Gidley, James Williams, and Frederic B. Loomis

1926   Fossil Man in Florida. *American Journal of Science*, 5th series 12(69):254–264.

Giles, Eugene, and Orville Elliot

1962   Race Identification from Cranial Measurements. *Journal of Forensic Sciences* 7(2):147–157.

Hann, John H.
  1990 De Soto, Dobyns, and Demography in Western Timucua. *The Florida Anthropologist* 43:3–12.
Holmes, W. H.
  1918 On the Antiquity of Man in America. *Science* 47(1223):561–562.
  1925 The Antiquity Phantom in American Archeology. *Science* 62(1603):256–258.
Hrdlička, Aleš
  1901 A Painted Skeleton from Northern Mexico, with Notes on Bone Painting among the American Aborigines. *American Anthropologist* 3:701–725.
  1902 The Aztecs of Yesterday and Today. *Harper's* 106:37–42.
  1903 The Region of the Ancient "Chichimecs," with Notes on the Tepecanos and the Ruin of La Quemada, Mexico. *American Anthropologist* 5:385–440.
  1907 *Skeletal Remains Suggesting or Attributed to Early Man in North America.* Bulletin 33. Bureau of American Ethnology, Smithsonian Institution, Washington, D.C.
  1908 *Physiological and Medical Observations Among the Indians of Southwestern United States and Northern Mexico.* Bulletin 34. Bureau of American Ethnology, Smithsonian Institution, Washington, D.C.
  1909 *Tuberculosis Among Certain Indian Tribes of the United States.* Bulletin 42. Bureau of American Ethnology, Smithsonian Institution, Washington, D.C.
  1912 *Early Man in South America.* Bulletin 52. Bureau of American Ethnology, Smithsonian Institution, Washington, D.C.
  1916 *Physical Anthropology of the Lenape or Delawares, and of the Eastern Indians in General.* Bulletin 62. Bureau of American Ethnology, Smithsonian Institution, Washington, D.C.
  1917a Preliminary Report on Finds of Supposedly Ancient Human Re-

mains at Vero, Florida. *Journal of Geology* 25(1):43–51.

1917b Trip to Fort Myers Region, West Coast of Florida. *Smithsonian Miscellaneous Collections* 66(17):28–29.

1918a Expedition Notes (in Notebook labeled "Fla. 1918"). Papers of Aleš Hrdlička, Box 92. National Anthropological Archives, Smithsonian Institution, Washington, D.C.

1918b *Recent Discoveries Attributed to Early Man in America.* Bulletin 66. Bureau of American Ethnology, Smithsonian Institution, Washington, D.C.

1919 Anthropological Survey of the Southwestern Coast of Florida. *Smithsonian Miscellaneous Collections* 70(2):62–65.

1922 *The Anthropology of Florida.* Publications of the Florida State His-
[2007] torical Society, DeLand.

1932 Letter to Ernest F. Coe, dated December 8. Ms. on file, Marjory Stoneman Douglas Papers, Richter Library, University of Miami, Coral Gables.

1937 Early Man in America: What Have the Bones to Say? In *Early Man as Depicted by Leading Authorities at the International Symposium on Early Man, the Academy of Natural Sciences, Philadelphia, March 1937,* edited by George Grant MacCurdy, pp. 93–104. Peabody Museum of American Archaeology and Ethnology, Harvard University, Cambridge.

1940 Catalog of Human Crania in the United States National Museum Collections: Indians of the Gulf States. *Proceedings of the United States National Museum* 87:315–364.

Judd, Neil M.

1967 *The Bureau of American Ethnology: A Partial History.* University of Oklahoma Press, Norman.

Kolianos, Phyllis E., and Brent R. Weisman (editors)

2005a *The Florida Journals of Frank Hamilton Cushing.* University Press of Florida, Gainesville.

2005b *The Lost Florida Manuscript of Frank Hamilton Cushing.* University Press of Florida, Gainesville.

Lane, Ed

1998 *The Florida Geological Survey—An Illustrated Chronicle and Brief History.* Special Publication No. 42. Florida Geological Survey, Tallahassee.

Loomis, F. B.

1924 Artifacts Associated with the Remains of a Columbian Elephant at Melbourne, Florida. *American Journal of Science,* 5th series 8(48):503–508.

1925 The Florida Man. *Science* 62(1611):436.

1926 Early Man in Florida. *Natural History* 26(3):260–262.

Lumholtz, C., and Aleš Hrdlička

1898 Marked Human Bones from a Prehistoric Tarasco Indian Burial-place in the State of Michoacan, Mexico. *Bulletin of the American Museum of Natural History* 10:61–79.

Marquardt, William H. (editor)

1992 *Culture and Environment in the Domain of the Calusa.* Monograph 1. Institute of Archaeology and Paleoenvironmental Studies, Department of Anthropology, Florida Museum of Natural History, Gainesville.

Meltzer, David J.

1991 On "Paradigms" and "Paradigm Bias" in Controversies Over Human Antiquity in America. In *The First Americans: Search and Research,* edited by Tom D. Dillehay and David J. Meltzer, pp. 13–49. CRC Press, Boca Raton, Florida.

1994 The Discovery of Deep Time: A History of Views on the Peopling of the Americas. In *Method and Theory for Investigating the Peopling of the Americas,* edited by Robson Bonnichsen and D. Gentry Steele, pp. 7–26. Center for the Study of the First Americans, Oregon State University, Corvallis.

Meltzer, David J., and Robert C. Dunnell
  1992 Introduction. In *The Archaeology of William Henry Holmes*, edited by David J. Meltzer and Robert C. Dunnell, pp. vii-l. Smithsonian Institution Press, Washington, D.C.

Milanich, Jerald T.
  1987 Corn and Calusa: De Soto and Demography. In *Coasts, Plains and Deserts: Essays in Honor of Reynold J. Ruppé*, edited by Sylvia W. Gaines, pp. 173–184. Anthropological Research Papers No. 38. Arizona State University, Tempe.
  1994 *Archaeology of Precolumbian Florida*. University Press of Florida, Gainesville.

Mitchem, Jeffrey M. (editor)
  1999 *The West and Central Florida Expeditions of Clarence Bloomfield Moore*. The University of Alabama Press, Tuscaloosa.

Montagu, M. F. Ashley
  1944 Aleš Hrdlička, 1869–1943. *American Anthropologist* 46:113–117.

Montgomery, Robert Lynn
  1996 *Register to the Papers of Aleš Hrdlička*. National Anthropological Archives, Smithsonian Institution, Washington, D.C.

Moore, Clarence B.
  1900 Certain Antiquities of the Florida West-Coast. *Journal of the Academy of Natural Sciences of Philadelphia* 11:350–394.
  1905 Miscellaneous Investigation in Florida. *Journal of the Academy of Natural Sciences of Philadelphia* 13:298–325.
  1907 Notes on the Ten Thousand Islands, Florida. *Journal of the Academy of Natural Sciences of Philadelphia* 13:457–470.

Phillips, Philip
  1973 Introduction. In *The Archaeological Reports of Frederic Ward Putnam: Selected from the Annual Reports of the Peabody Museum of Archaeology and Ethnology, Harvard University, 1875–1903*, edited by Philip

Phillips, pp. ix–xii. AMS Press, New York.

Prokopec, M.
1991   Hrdlička, Aleš. In *International Dictionary of Anthropologists*, edited by Christopher Winters, pp. 310–312. Translated by June Pachuta Farris. Garland Press, New York.

Schultz, Adolph H.
1944   Biographical Memoir of Aleš Hrdlička, 1869–1943. *Biographical Memoirs* XXIII(12). National Academy of Sciences, Washington, D.C.

Sellards, Elias H.
1916a Human Remains from the Pleistocene of Florida. *Science* 44(1139): 615–617.
1916b On the Discovery of Fossil Human Remains in Florida in Association with Extinct Vertebrates. *American Journal of Science*, 4th series 42(247):1–18.
1917a Further Notes on Human Remains from Vero, Florida. *American Anthropologist* 19(2):239–251.
1917b On the Association of Human Remains and Extinct Vertebrates at Vero, Florida. *Journal of Geology* 25(1):4–24.

Shofner, Jerrell H.
2004   *The Florida Historical Society, 1856–2004*. Florida Historical Society Press, Cocoa.

Spencer, Frank
1979   "Aleš Hrdlička, M.D., 1869–1943: A Chronicle of the Life and Work of an American Physical Anthropologist." 2 vols. Unpublished doctoral dissertation, Department of Anthropology, University of Michigan, Ann Arbor.

Stetson, John B., Jr.
1923   Letter to Herman Gunter, dated August 20. Ms. on file, Florida Geological Survey Archives, Microfilm reel 112. Tallahassee.

Stewart, T. D.
  1940   The Life and Writings of Dr. Aleš Hrdlička (1869–1939). *American Journal of Physical Anthropology* 26:3–40.
Widmer, Randolph E.
  1988   *The Evolution of the Calusa: A Nonagricultural Chiefdom on the Southwest Florida Coast.* The University of Alabama Press, Tuscaloosa.
Wilmsen, Edwin N.
  1965   An Outline of Early Man Studies in the United States. *American Antiquity* 31(2):172–192.

INDEX TO THE INTRODUCTION

ANTHROPOLOGY

OF

FLORIDA

ANTHROPOLOGY OF FLORIDA

CONTENTS

I

INDIAN REMAINS OF THE SOUTHWESTERN COAST OF FLORIDA

II

ANTHROPOLOGY OF FLORIDA

III

NEW OBSERVATIONS

ILLUSTRATIONS

FOREWORD

WHEN at the end of October, 1918, shortly after the death of my wife, Professor W. H. Holmes and Dr. J. W. Fewkes, through the Bureau of American Ethnology, offered me the facilities for a brief trip of exploration, I chose one of the least known regions in the States, namely, the southwestern extremity of Florida. I have been in Florida on anthropological quests on three other occasions, reaching on the west coast as far south as Fort Myers; this time I wanted to penetrate as far south as there might be traces of the former aboriginal population, to get a rapid bird's-eye view of conditions, to collect whatever skeletal material I might be able to find, and to see as many as possible of the Seminoles who are known to roam through that territory. I was aware, of course, of the work of Mr. Clarence B. Moore, as well as of that of Hamilton Cushing, along that coast; but for purposes of physical anthropology that was not enough, and I felt a strong need of a personal visit to these regions.

The trip proved interesting, though also difficult, beyond all expectation. The region contains a wealth of archeological remains which would long since have created quite a stir if located in a more accessible part of the country. It also contains burials, probably many burials, of the old population; but it soon appeared that nothing of these skeletal remains has been saved by any one of the few local settlers, and that nothing could be excavated on the trip, due to unpropitious season with swarms of insects and a complete lack of help. Of the Seminoles a few only were met; to seek the rest was out of the question.

The results of the journey as marked on the spot are given in the following pages, with the hope that they may supplement and advance Mr. Moore's work and reports. The physical anthropology of this part of the peninsula, together with that of the southeastern coast, must remain, in the main, for future determination.

The second part of this memoir will be devoted to a study of the Florida natives from the rest of the peninsula.[1] Due to their geographical position and other facts, this study has long been felt to be desirable, but it was only in the last few years that enough skeletal material was obtained both from Florida and from neighboring States to make possible some valid general deductions. We owe this again, it may be acknowledged with pleasure, mainly to Mr. Clarence B. Moore's painstaking explorations in Georgia, Arkansas and Louisiana, as well as Florida.

The results of the studies here dealt with, together with those on tribes further north and west, lead to a strong hope that if these researches can be properly extended, particularly to the Northwest and to Mexico, we may before long be able fairly to master the intricate subject of the types and relations of the North-American Indians.

[1] The completion of this study, also, has been made possible by a small grant from the Bureau of American Ethnology, to which the author hereby gratefully acknowledges his indebtedness.

I

NOTES ON THE INDIAN REMAINS OF THE SOUTHWESTERN COAST OF FLORIDA

THE Ten Thousand Islands Region.—Of the few as yet but very imperfectly explored regions in the United States, the largest perhaps is the southernmost part of Florida below the 26th degree of northern latitude. This is particularly true of the central and western portions of this region, which inland are an unmapped wilderness of everglades and cypress swamps, and off-shore a maze of low mangrove "keys" or islands, mostly unnamed and uncharted, with channels, "rivers" and "bays" about them which are known only to a few of the trappers and hunters who have lived a larger part of their life in that region. The islands are literally numbered by the thousands, and range in size from a little oyster bar with perhaps a single little mangrove, to those which measure several square miles of surface. They are invariably thickly wooded by the almost impenetrable, many-rooted, tough mangrove brush or trees, a jungle-like vegetation which constitutes one of the greatest obstacles to exploration. All these islands, moreover, are so low that they are practically nothing but muck and swamp with parts covered with water at high tide and the whole surface submerged when western storms drive in the Gulf sea. They are uninhabited and uninhabitable by man except where the gulf, winds, or human hands had built some "high ground," on which the Indians and now the whites with some degree of safety erect their habitations.

In addition to the swampy and jungly nature of these islands, which is such that except on the "high ground" it is impossible to find a place for a camp and in most places even for the cooking of a meal, these patches together with the neighboring mainland are more or less infested with snakes and the larger part of the year also with great quantities of mosquitoes, sandflies, and "red bugs," which make life and frequently even a short stay on them a matter of torture and even danger. Under such circumstances anything like a detailed, protracted exploration is not merely exceptionally difficult but frequently quite impossible.

On such maps as we have of this region, the innumerable mangrove "keys" are known by the well fitting term of the "Ten Thousand Islands." The waters that surround them are full of submerged oyster bars, and frequently so shallow that only the lightest draft launches or skiffs can penetrate; while distances with directions are merely a matter of individual estimates or approximations by the hunters and trappers of the region. As one nears the mainland, some of the more important waterways begin to be called "rivers" and "bays"; and if the former are followed one actually enters sooner or later freshwater rivers, which run, gradually petering out, for from a few to a dozen or more miles inland, draining the low Everglades.

Due to the above-named conditions the whole region of the "Ten Thousand Islands" is but very sparsely peopled and with the exception of a few store and hotel keepers (the latter essentially for the accommodation of the occasional visiting sportsmen), it is inhabited only by a scattering of fishermen, most of whom also hunt and trap on occasion. From Chocaloskee Island down to the southernmost point of Cape Sable, a distance along the shore of over fifty miles, the actual settlers were found to consist of only five or six families.

From the archeological point of view, the region of the "Ten Thousand Islands", together with the adjacent coast, first became known through the work of Frank Hamilton Cushing in 1895–97.[1] Subsequently this region, as practically all other parts of the west coast of Florida, was visited on several occasions by Mr. Clarence B. Moore. These visits, as all of Mr. Moore's work, were also of archeological nature, and resulted in the collection of numerous interesting cultural specimens which are described and illustrated in Vols. XI and XIII of the Journal of the Philadelphia Academy of Sciences, and deposited in the collections of the Academy.

Mr. Moore's observations, as far as they extend, are just, and except so far as they apply to descriptions of specimens, deserve to be quoted in full. They are as follows:[2]

"The Ten Thousand Islands, whose name is not conferred in a poetical way, but probably falls short in describing the number, beginning with Little Marco Island on the north, thickly fringe the coast line of part of the counties of Lee and Monroe to the Northwest Cape, a distance of about seventy miles in a straight line.

"These keys, formed by oyster bars, sand and the roots of the mangrove tree, are from a few feet to a number of miles in area, and are, as a rule, just above the level of the sea. But an insignificant proportion of these islands have been utilized by the Key-dwellers.

"All published maps of this part of Florida are grossly inaccurate. . . .

"On the eastern side of Little Marco Island is a shell settlement with the usual ridges and mounds of moderate size.

---

[1] Exploration of Ancient Key-dweller Remains in the Gulf Coast of Florida. *Proc. Amer. Philos. Soc.*, 1897, xxxv, 120 pp.

[2] Certain Antiquities of the Florida West Coast. *J. Ac. Sc.*, Philadelphia, 1900, xi, 369 et seq.

"Marco, on the northernmost end of Key Marco, by far the most important of the Ten Thousand Islands, is where Mr. Cushing made his marvellous collection of objects of wood and of shell in the muck at the bottom of a small triangular court enclosed between ridges of shell. . . .

"Blue Hill, on Horr's Island, about one mile southwest from Goodland Point, has a considerable aboriginal shell deposit, and a sand mound about 6 feet in height, which has been thoroughly dug through.

"Caximbas Hill is a wind formation on the southwestern part of Marco Island. Nearby is a considerable shell deposit.

"Proceeding in a southerly direction among the Ten Thousand Islands, we visited Gomez' Old Place on a small nameless key reached from the Gulf through a pass about two miles east of Coon Key, and continuing in about one mile in a northerly direction. The key at present writing (1900) is uninhabited. It covers probably about thirty acres of interesting shell deposit, partly surrounding a basin that fills with the rising tide.

"Dismal Key, Lee County, lies about two miles north of Horse Key, an outside island about five miles E. S. E. from Coon Key Pass, which is the southern entrance to Marco. This unsurveyed key has a great shell deposit with the usual mounds and the like.

"Fikahatchee Key, Lee County, unsurveyed, perhaps 150 acres in extent, can be reached by an inland passage at high tide, or from the Gulf through a nameless pass and continuing in among the islands for from three to four miles. In any event, a pilot is requisite. On this island is an extensive shell deposit. A family living on the key occupies a house partly built upon piles.

"Russell's Key may be reached from the Gulf by entering the islands about three miles above Sandfly Pass and continuing in among the keys another three miles. This key, which has large aboriginal shell deposits, perhaps 60 acres in extent, is occupied by Mr. J. W. Russell and Mr. M. M. Gaston with their families.

"Wiggins' Key on Sandfly Pass, about one mile from the Gulf, on the right-hand side going out, has extensive shell deposits and two small burial mounds of sand and shell which have been much dug into. Our excavations, made with permission of Mr. J. Wiggins, the owner, were unrewarded.

"This place is shown on maps as in the northern limits of the County of Monroe, but at the present time this territory, extending south below Chokoloskee Key, is claimed by Lee County, and, it is said, probably will be obtained by it.

"Chokoloskee Key, Monroe County. This island lies in the lower part of Chokoloskee Bay, a sheet of water back of the maze of islands bordering the Gulf.

"The island is unsurveyed. It is roughly circular and is said to be somewhat over one-half mile in diameter. It is almost entirely covered with great shell deposits, including lofty peaks, graded ways, canals and the like. Rising from the mangrove swamp at the edge of the northern part of the island is a mound of shell of abrupt ascent, a fraction over 27 feet in height, if measured from the level of low water. Running in from the southern section of the island are two graded ways enclosing a canal. These ways terminate in mounds facing each other. The easternmost mound, slightly the higher, on its western side where it rises from the canal, has a slope of thirty-three degrees. Its height above the level of the bottom of the canal is 18 feet 4 inches and 22 feet 4 inches above low water level. . . .

"Near the mouth of Turner's River, which enters Choko-loskee Bay in an easterly direction from the key and not far from it, is a considerable shell deposit. . . .

"Watson's, Monroe County. About four miles up Chatham River is a series of shell fields owned by Mr. Watson, who resides on the place."

To which, in 1905,[1] Mr. Moore adds the following:

"This season (1904), beginning at Charlotte Harbor, we con-tinued southward through Pine Island Sound, Estero Bay and along the Gulf coast to the island of Marco next to the northern-most key of the Ten Thousand Islands. From Key Marco our course lay through the keys including Chokoloskee Key and Lossman's Key, and along the coast to Cape Sable, the southern boundary of the Ten Thousand Islands.

"Rounding Cape Sable and visiting points of interest on the mainland and investigating various keys, we continued eastward, then northward, to Miami; to Fort Lauderdale on New River, where the Everglades were visited; and finally to Lake Worth, which was the southern limit of our work during the season of 1896.

"As a result of this part of our journey of the season of 1904, we formed certain conclusions, and fortified others which we had previously expressed in print, namely:

"(1) That while the shell deposits of the southwestern coast of Florida are of great interest as monuments of the aborigines, their contents offer little reward to the investigator.

"(2) That the sand mounds of the southern Florida coast were built mainly for domiciliary purposes, and that such as contain burials yield but little pottery, whole vessels being practically absent.

---

[1] Miscellaneous Investigations in Florida. *J. Ac. Sc.*, Philadelphia, 1905–08, xiii, 303 et seq.

"(3) That these burial mounds contain but few artifacts of interest and that such artifacts as are met with in the smaller ones, and superficially in the larger ones, are often of European origin, marking a strong contrast with the mounds of the northwestern Florida coast and of St. John's River.

"The Marco Key, where Cushing made his great collection, was revisited. The objects found by Cushing lay in muck which forms the bottom of a small artificial basin in the shell deposit, formerly connected by a short canal with the neighboring water. . . . Artificial harbors, basins and canals abound among such keys of the Ten Thousand Islands as were selected by the pile dwellers as places of residence. . . .

"The interesting Chokoloskee Key described in our previous report has been determined, by a recent survey, to be in Lee County, and not in Monroe County, as was formerly believed to be the case. . . .

"In one part of the key is an interesting artificial harbor which, no doubt, served as a shelter for canoes in aboriginal times. This harbor, protected from open water by an embankment of shell, save at a narrow entrance, was on property owned by Mr. McKinnery, who, controlling the water by the insertion of a sluice, dug many trenches in the muck, with the idea to pile this material above water level, and thus gain a rich area for cultivation. . . .

"Lossman's Key, Monroe County. After investigating a number of keys which yielded nothing of interest from an archeological point of view, Lossman's Key, one of the largest, if not the largest key of the Ten Thousand Islands, was visited. At the northern extremity are large, level causeways and platforms of shell, a thorough survey of which would be of interest.

"South of Cape Sable and eastward among the keys and northward to Lake Worth, where our journey ended, we met with nothing of especial archeological interest. After leaving the Ten Thousand Islands, no shell keys were met with by us during an extended search, all islands being of sand or of limerock."

And again in 1907:[1]

"The Ten Thousand Islands which have been twice visited and twice written about by us were again the subject of our investigation during two seasons, the winter of 1906 and the winter of 1907. These islands fringe the coast of south-western Florida for about 80 miles along parts of the counties of Lee and Monroe, between the settlement known as Naples on the north and Cape Sable on the south. . . .

"While at Marco we visited Little Marco; McIlvaine's Key; Addison's Key; and the Crawford place, northward toward Naples—all noteworthy aboriginal shell deposits. . . .

"Fikahatchee Key and Russell's Key, large shell islands, yielded specimens of aboriginal work. Chokoloskee Key was visited with good results. . . .

"Lossman's Key, near Cape Sable, one of the largest keys of the Ten Thousand Islands, was again visited by us, and its two shell deposits—one more than ten acres in extent—were carefully examined. The larger deposit, rich in aboriginal implements, has been recently cleared of the hammock growth formerly upon it. While there we almost walked upon the wires of a loaded spring-gun set for deer or panther—one of the chances one takes in exploring this wild and lawless region."

The rest of the paper is given to description of objects.

A copy of the notes on the principal observations by the writer was sent to Mr. Moore soon after the writer's return from

[1] Notes on the Ten Thousand Islands, Florida. *J. Ac. Sc.*, Philadelphia, xiii, 458 et seq.

Florida, and a preliminary note on the trip was published in the popular "Smithsonian Explorations" for 1918. In 1919 Mr. Moore visited once more a part of this coast, and in the last number of the American Anthropologist of that year (p. 400 et seq.), referring to the above mentioned note, he states in the main as follows

Our "hundred-foot steamer, carrying a power boat as a tender, with an average of eleven men to dig and to supervise, has spent much of five seasons in the Ten Thousand Islands, good parts of which were devoted to the region south of Key Marco, in one instance the expedition continuing around the end of the peninsula to Lake Worth on the eastern coast.

"We have published the results of most of our investigations between Key Marco and Lossman's Key, the southernmost of the Ten Thousand Islands, including principal sites, Dismal Key, Fikahatchee Key, Russell's Key, Chokoloskee Key, Turner River and Lossman's Key.

"We are not prepared to admit that *the region of the coast south of Key Marco was supposed to be of no great account as far as aboriginal remains were concerned* by anyone familiar with that region through personal investigation or through comprehensive reading on the subject. Nor, on the other hand, is it our opinion that this region is more than a continuation of the great shell deposits farther north: The huge mound above Cedar Key; those at Cedar Key; the so-called Spanish mound, Crystal River; Indian Hill, on Tampa Bay; Josselyn Key; the Battey Place, now Pineland on Pine Island; Mound Island; Addison's Key; Goodland Point on Key Marco; and others, all of which we have carefully examined and nearly all described in print. The highest shell-mounds of the coast are north of Key Marco as is the best defined aboriginal canal.

"Our own experience and that of others has convinced us that in the shell-heaps of the southwestern Florida coast, which extend southward from above Cedar Key, practically nothing of interest has been found that can begin to compensate one for the heavy outlay of time and money needed for their demolition. The great shell-mound on Bullfrog creek, ten miles southeast from Tampa, removed to furnish material for roads, was carefully watched, it is said, while the work was going on, without any discovery of importance. An accurate survey of the shell site on Turner River might be of interest, but it is our belief that digging into the shell deposits hereafter will be more frequently suggested than done."

So much for Mr. Moore's report.

The writer's motives for a visit to this region were, as already mentioned, besides its character, a desire to satisfy himself as to the nature and promise from the point of physical anthropology of the numerous remains of Indian occupation along the coast from Charlotte Bay southward; to determine if possible the type of skeletal remains from Key Marco down to the tip of the peninsula, for purposes of comparison with those which on previous trips he saw or collected off the Caloosahatchee River and further northward along the coast; and finally a hope of finding some full-blood Seminoles, parties of whom were known to roam among the Ten Thousand Islands. An additional incentive for the visit to southern Florida was to visit the newly opened regions about Lake Okechobee, where many canals have been and are being constructed, to see if any discoveries had been made there which might possibly throw light on the nature and antiquity of the inhabitants of that territory.

Due to special good fortune the whole trip was accomplished within the time of four weeks, the main part of which was devoted to a journey of about 250 miles, with a small launch and a skiff, through the islands from Key Marco south to Lossman's River. One of the most experienced and reliable guides of the region was secured in the person of "Uncle" James E. Cannon, of Marco; and a number of friendly, remarkably well-informed and reliable old settlers were found in the persons of Messrs. J. B. Ellis, George W. Storter, C. S. Smallwood and R. E. Hamilton, from whom valuable information was obtained, a service which is hereby gratefully acknowledged. The expedition was also favored by excellent weather; but the insects proved a most difficult proposition, and in many cases not only made a prolonged examination of the remains impossible, but rendered also all exploratory digging out of question. It was often difficult, in fact, to secure even a general view of the remains and to make a few photographic exposures. Due to these and other impediments, a good many of the less important sites and mounds that were learned of were not visited, and their location and character can only be recorded on the basis of the information obtained from the above-named settlers; but all groups that were regarded as of more than common interest or promise were reached and as far as possible examined.

During these examinations much was seen that has not yet been recorded in print. Mr. Clarence B. Moore, who saw many of these sites before, in mentioning them did not go, as was seen, into many details. Yet there are details which seemed worth while recording even though very imperfectly, before the various remains will be more or less obliterated by man who even in these regions is advancing and destroying. Already some of the sites, such as that on the Chokaloskee Island, are badly damaged.

To facilitate description the report on what was learned will best be divided into four portions, namely: (1) The Indian remains from Fort Myers to Key Marco; (2) The Indian remains from Key Marco to the southern extremity of the peninsula; (3) The Indian remains in the region from Fort Myers to Lake Okechobee, and from the latter to the east coast; and (4) The Seminole Indians.

INDIAN REMAINS FROM FORT MYERS TO KEY MARCO

As is well known, the islands lying south of Charlotte Harbor and S. W. of the mouth of the Caloosahatchee, as well as some neighboring parts of the mainland, contain many Indian remains in the way of shell heaps, sand mounds, etc. They have also yielded considerable skeletal material, only a small part of which was, however, preserved. The main of these have been at least partly explored and reported upon (Cushing,[1] Clarence B. Moore,[2] Hrdlička[3]). For some distance south of the mouth of the Caloosahatchee River such remains become scarcer and less well known. Commencing at the Punta Rasa and southward they may, so far as present information goes, be briefly enumerated as follows:

Punta Rasa: According to the Captains Kinzie of Fort Myers, there is a good-sized sand mound with burials in the swamps inland from Punta Rasa. Mr. C. B. Moore, to whom the writer mentioned this mound, wrote that he knew of it, and that some of the burials which it contained were accompanied by beads of white man's manufacture. None of the skeletal remains have, so far as could be learned, been preserved.

Estero Keys: West of Estero (10 miles S. of Fort Myers,) there is a shallow, wide-mouthed bay with a series of keys and islands, some of which contain Indian remains. The most important of these is the "Mound Key," with extensive shell

---

[1] O. c.
[2] O. c.
[3] Bulls. 33 and 66, Bureau American Ethnology.

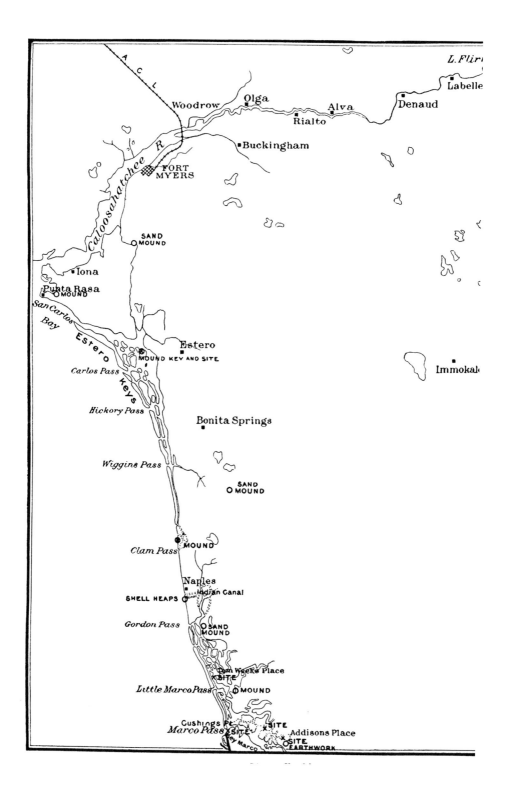

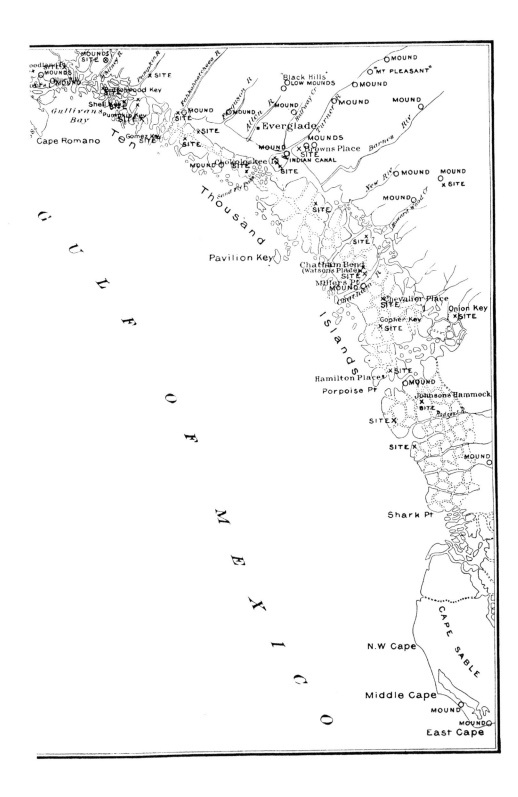

heaps and mounds which were partly touched upon by Cushing,[1] and later described more accurately though not exhaustively by Clarence B. Moore.[2]

It would seem that the remains of this little archipelago and particularly those of Mound Key deserve further attention. The region is easily approachable from Fort Myers or Estero. No skeletal material is as yet known from these islands.

Fort Myers-Naples: More inland, the country here is, in general, very unproductive. It is covered with a thin pine forest, the grass is poor and the region could never have furnished the means of existence to any large Indian population. It shows accordingly but few marks of such occupation. These consist of two moderate sized sand mounds, in all probability containing burials, situated one about six miles south of Fort Myers and not far east of the road to Naples, at the head of Hender's Creek; while the other is to be found about six miles southeast of Bonita Springs (or about twenty-seven miles from Fort Myers). This latter mound lies to the east of the road to Naples, in the pine forest, and in one locality can be seen from the present road.

Naples: About thirty-five miles in a straight line and nearly due south from Fort Myers is the little hamlet of Naples. Approximately four miles north of Naples, in the neighborhood of "Clam Pass," there are, according to information, shell-and-soil mounds or heaps, some reaching possibly 15 feet in height and the total covering upwards of 2 acres. To find them one would "go up the Pass and enter a little bay, on the north side of which the site may readily be seen." This information is rather uncertain, but there were no facilities to visit the location.

---

[1] O. c.
[2] O. c.

A short distance to the S. E. of Naples exists an old canal which originally led from the "back bay" to the Gulf, and which may be a work of the Indians among whom canals facilitating canoe approach to their sites were greatly favored. Some low shell accumulations are said to be found near the Gulf extremity of the canal, the mouth of which is reported to be now about 70 yards distant from the beach.

Gordon Pass: To the southeast of Naples there is a fairly spacious shallow inland bay, to the west of which is placed by some the northern beginning of the "Ten Thousand Islands." A small sound about 4 miles south of Naples and communicating with the Gulf is known as the "Gordon Pass"; and almost opposite this Pass on the mainland to the east is a good-sized oblong sand mound, from which human bones and some "cement" have been dug up by local men. The mound is situated about half a mile inland, on the western side of a pond and not far from a "slew" which leads from the pond to a swamp located between it and the bay. This site was visited and our little party proceeded up to the "slew," which may possibly be another old Indian canal, but there our further progress was blocked by water which we were not able to pass.

Tom Weeks' Place: About 7 miles southeast of Naples and on the "river" between Naples and Marco, is Crawford's Key, now better known as the "Tom Weeks' Place," and sometimes also called the "Shell Key." The site is mentioned by Mr. Moore as having been seen by him and containing "noteworthy aboriginal shell deposits" (p. 12). There is an old, abandoned house on this place with a dilapidated landing; and there are upwards of 4 acres of "high land," which on a visit proved to consist of six large, oblong heaps and mounds, with some additional artificially made ground in the vicinity. The highest of the mounds is located near the middle of the small island, is at least 15 feet high, and covers probably half an acre of ground. All of these heaps are made up of shells, though they also contain more or less black soil (muck and sand). The surface of a part of the high ground has been affected by plowing, but there was no evidence of any excavation. The whole is plainly a village site, the shell heaps having served as elevated platforms for habitations; and it impresses one as rather sterile, so far as relics and skeletal remains are concerned, in which, however, it would be easy to be mistaken.

Key Marco: A little over 12 miles S. E. of Naples is the large Key Marco, one of the best known points archeologically on the western Florida coast, thanks especially to Cushing's explorations. Mr. Moore mentions the Key (pp. 8-13) but does not seem to have made any special explorations there. On the site explored by Cushing, near the northeastern extremity of the Key, matters are very much as he left them, the main depression where he made his great finds forming now an unattractive and unimpressive pool filled with dark brown water. A casual examination of the ground in the vicinity indicates that a large part of this northwestern extremity of the island was, and to some extent still is covered by Indian shell heaps and accumulations. It was undoubtedly an important and extensive Indian site, though as learned later on by no means the most important of the western coast, except for Cushing's discoveries. It had been so affected by removal of shell and the activities of the adjoining settlement that little of value could now be said about it. Indian remains on the Marco Key are, however, not limited to the point just mentioned and which would seem to deserve the name of "Cushing's Point." The term "pile-dwellers" applied by Cushing to the aboriginal inhabitants of this point seems unmerited. Cushing's important collection of skulls of this place could so far, regrettably, not be located. (Ultimate inquiries make it probable that there were but a few specimens).

Caximbas: Five miles southwest of Marco is the settlement of Caximbas. Mr. Moore refers briefly to this site; the place is now owned by Mr. J. M. Barfield. There are on the property approximately 20 acres of ground made by the Indians, and Mr. Barfield kindly conveyed the writer over this ground. This has been considerably affected by cultivation, but it is evident that it was an extensive and important Indian settlement. Much of the land seems to have been made for the purposes of agriculture, while other parts served as platforms for habitations. There are several trough-like depressions leading from between the heaps in the direction of the water outside the key; they served in all probability for approach by canoes. The land is sand mixed with muck and contains many conch, clam and oyster shells. Many of the conchs show the characteristic hole made by the Indians and some a double hole for hefting. Fragments of undecorated pottery are common. No burial place, or any extraordinary objects such as those found by Cushing further north, have as yet come to light at Caximbas.

Further inland there are large shell deposits which are doubtless also of Indian origin. Finally near the shore there is a high and long sand ridge, the Caximba "hill," a unique occurrence in the Ten Thousand Islands and an excellent site for Mr. Barfield's hotel; the indications are that it is a sand dune the formation of which was favored by a peculiar exposure towards the Gulf.

Horr's Island: Opposite Caximbas on the south and across a moderately wide sound lies the as yet ill-mapped Horr's Island, so named after Captain J. F. Horr, who very kindly conducted the writer to his place and showed him the Indian remains that are found on the same. These consist of three shell and one sand mound.

The first of the shell mounds is situated about 700 feet east by north from the house. It is bluntly conical, between 4 and 5 feet high, but originally was somewhat higher—perhaps a little over 5 feet, and at the base is about 40 feet in diameter. It has not as yet been dug into.

The second and largest of the three shell mounds is situated about 300 feet farther in the same direction. It is somewhat oblong, approximately 20 feet high and upwards of 80 feet in maximum diameter. A great deal of shell has been removed from this mound for roads, and during this work various archeological objects were discovered, including two finely polished "banner stones," one of which was still in Captain Horr's possession at the time of the writer's visit. They were unquestionably of much more northern origin. It is not known if any human bones were ever encountered in the mound, but if so they were inconspicuous. Several pieces of glass were, however, found among the shells, showing white man's contact.

The third shell mound is located about half a mile (local estimate) east of the one just mentioned. It is conical, smaller than the big mound, and located on higher ground. Some shells were taken from the edge of it, but the work did not penetrate very far and no finds are remembered.

On the eastern end of Horr's Island, or about 2 miles from the present house and a short distance from where the old house stood, is a sand mound (see Mr. Moore's note, p. 8). The place is sometimes called "The Blue Hills," for which term, however, there seems to be little justification. It is possible that originally two sand mounds have existed in the locality; at present, however, there is but one, about 60 feet in diameter and perhaps 12 feet high, conical, but with the top cut off by some former excavation. The report is that these excavations had yielded human skulls and bones, and also some objects of white man's derivation.

Goodland Point: A little over three miles S. E. from Caximbas, or 6½ miles S. S. E. from Marco, other extensive Indian remains in the way of shell heaps, canals, and mounds with burials occur on the so-called Goodland Point, the whole covering many acres of ground. Not far from the house of the present inhabitants on the Point and between two large shell ridges there remains a short canal, doubtless partly or entirely of Indian making, which is usable to this day for small boats. This place was visited by Mr. Clarence B. Moore, who conducted here some excavations that yielded archeological specimens as well as human bones, but nothing of great importance. He barely mentions it (p. 13). It would seem to deserve a comprehensive survey. The amount of shell heaps and made ground is imposing.

Cape Romaine: The large key which terminates in Cape Romaine, S. S. W. of Key Marco, has been unanimously reported to the writer as a low sandy beach, exposed to the storms of the Gulf and containing no Indian remains that had ever been noted.

Addison's Place: One of the most extensive and interesting Indian shell deposits, which belongs to the Marco group and should, therefore, be described in this connection, is to be found on the so-called "Addison's Place," on MacIlvaine Creek, approximately 5 miles east from Cushing's Point at Marco (Mr. Moore's notes, p. 12, 13). The moderate sized key on which the place is located seems to be without a fixed name. It is farmed by the good Addison family, a typical west Florida coast group of hard-working parents with many robust children, notwithstanding the mosquitoes; and it was Mrs. Addison with

PLATE I. Jungle near the Sand Mound, Horr's Island

two of her girls who piloted the writer over the highly interesting and vast Indian formations which cover practically the
whole island, which is about 30 acres in area. They consist of
great shell ridges arranged in a row. This row runs roughly east
and west (the ridges themselves pointing north and south), curving
a little about the east end of the island. Between each two
of the ridges is a large and deep trough which in all probability
in the time of the Indians was a canal connecting with the
water outside of the key; and in the midst of the large ridges
not far from the house the troughs form a triangular "heart-
like" depression not unlike a little central harbor or shelter.
The huge ridges which are probably over 15 feet high with
four times that breadth and many times that length, make
a deep impression on the observer, and the whole of the remains
on this key ought to be carefully mapped for archeological
record, which would possibly be worth more than the results
of excavations. Human burials have, as far as could be learned,
not yet been located on this island.

On a separate little key about a quarter of a mile further
east, which also belongs to the Addisons who have there their
grape fruit orchard, there are additional remarkable remains
of handwork of the Indians. The area of the key in question is
said to be about 3 acres. In its middle is a fresh water pond;
and all around this, to near the outer limits of the key, is Indian
made "high land" 3 to 6 feet high above high tide and built
of sandy muck with some shell addition. From the pond
a couple of "gulleys" lead in the direction of the outside water-
course without now quite reaching it; they look very much as
if they may have originally been channels of approach to the
sheltered lagoon. All this is from a description by Mr. Addison, for due to conditions of the tide the little island could not
be visited.

Human bones and numerous "relics" have been found on the Addison Place, and the same was visited by Mr. Moore, but no explorations of it were as yet undertaken. The family themselves dug up a large part of one of the shell heaps for the purpose of making lime, but as could be anticipated discovered nothing striking in the way of human artifacts, and there were no bones.

General Remarks: So much for the region from south of Fort Myers to Key Marco. It is seen to offer a number of points of decided interest to the archeologist and prospectively also to the anthropologist, in the extensive shell heaps and mounds on the Mound Key, Tom Weeks' Place, Cushing's Point (Marco), Caximbas, Goodland Point, and on the two keys belonging to Mr. Addison. The white sand mounds are said to stop a few miles south of Naples, but the only reason is that further south such sand would be very hard to obtain. The burial mound at "Blue Hills" on Horr's Island shows the same tendency and similar material. The place of the beach-sand mound is taken by the muck-sand-and-shell mounds, which occur as will be seen later on to the southern extremity of the peninsula. The shell heaps and shell mounds resemble closely some of those existing on the keys south of Charlotte Harbor and evidently belonged to people of the same culture. With the exception of Cushing's Point at Marco none of the remains have as yet received exhaustive survey or exploration, the main reason for which being that they yield generally rather poor returns for the work, in addition to which there is the damping influence of the frequent though possibly only superficial presence in these places of articles such as glass beads, which indicates that the Indian population which built these sites persisted until well after European contact had become established.

INDIAN REMAINS FROM KEY MARCO SOUTHWARD

From the southern extremity of Key Marco the Florida coast bends southeastward and describes an arc of a wide circle open towards the Gulf. The Gulf for many miles off the coast here is shallow and beset with dangerous reefs; and for miles between these shallows and the mainland the concavity of the bend of the coast is occupied by the chain or archipelago of the Ten Thousand Islands, which represent a new land in various phases of formation. The border of the mainland itself is cut into by a series of short and more or less unknown rivers and creeks, which run generally from a northeasterly or easterly direction and drain the cypress swamps and everglades of the interior.

These imperfectly known regions teem with insects and other pests, but also with fish, mollusks, water fowl and many land animals, which advantages of food must have outweighed the many disadvantages and dangers of the territory with the Indians. The evidence of this is preserved in numerous, and in places great and archeologically important, remains of these people.

The remains in question are of two or possibly three classes. The first are simple shell heaps, composed principally of oyster shells, with a larger or smaller admixture of conchs, a few clam shells, turtle shells and bones of fish and various game animals. These heaps contain none or but little sand or soil; they are generally in the form of more or less pronounced, extensive and generally parallel ridges, the troughs between which served frequently—if not invariably—as canals which facilitated the approach with canoes. They are from such evidence as could be gathered poor to almost sterile in archeological or skeletal remains of the Indians. Their rôle was doubtless in the main that of platforms for habitations and for protection against the overflowing waters during storms. They were built expressly for these purposes, and that partly of dead shells brought to the spot from the beach and the oyster bars, and partly by the refuse shells and bones of the habitations.

Besides these ridges there are found in this region occasional isolated good-sized shell mounds. These are usually oval, but may be almost circular in outline, have more or less conical form with blunt or flat top, and range from about ten to near thirty feet in height. The material of which they are built is much the same as that of the shell heaps. The object of these shell mounds has not been determined. It is possible that some served as points for observation, or signalling, or for ceremonial observances, and some perhaps also for habitations and burials. None of these mounds have apparently as yet been explored.

The third variety of Indian remains consists of blunt, conical mounds ranging from a few to upwards of 20 feet in height, and built, at least so far as external appearances indicate, principally of sandy muck and small rotten shells. It is not unlikely that in some of these mounds shell in larger quantities may be found in the interior, for muck and sand were materials much more difficult to obtain. These mounds contain possibly in many, if not all instances, burials, but they also have in no single instance as yet been explored and their contents remain unknown.

In addition, there occur in this region some of the before-mentioned low muck-and-shell heaps with burials; and in connection with several of the larger sites there are indications of ground made for cultivation.

Notwithstanding the visible importance of some of the sites and their great extent, discoveries of archeological specimens as well as those of skeletal remains have so far been few and of no special value. Fragments of kitchen pottery, generally undecorated, while not exactly common, are to be found everywhere, but complete vessels seem to be as yet unknown. The most common "relics" are the doubly perforated conchs which evidently were hafted and used for hammers, perforators of other conchs, hoes, and similar purposes; and shell sinkers for fish nets with which the aborigines were evidently well acquainted. Stone objects, barring a rare importation, seem absent altogether; there is no stone in these regions from which they could have been manufactured.

Nearly all the important sites were personally visited, and although nothing like a satisfactory survey was in any case possible on account of the insects and other insurmountable impediments, some notes could, nevertheless, be made on the spot which may help to give a general idea of conditions and be of use to future explorers. In detail, the remains in question were found to be as follows:

Whitney River: Whitney River is a charming hidden stream of brown clear water, rich in fish. Its mouth is located to the S. E. E. and not far from the southernmost point of Key Marco. Its banks to the water edge are thickly overgrown with mangrove and other vegetation, which during our visit was studded here and there and enlivened by water fowl of pure white, rosy, blue and white or blue-gray plumage. There are no inhabitants along the stream and no traces of any white man ever having lived there formerly. It is one of the few places missed even by Mr. Moore's "Gopher."

About 5 miles from the mouth of the river—but one is never sure about these mouths—on the northern bank of the southern branch of the stream and about 50 feet from the water's edge, in swampy woods, there is a row of highly interesting and promising Indian mounds, and of elevated platforms for habitations.

The first mound as one proceeds up the river is a well-shaped, typical, conical heap, about 15 to 20 feet high and perhaps 60 feet in diameter, built of sandy muck, rotten oyster shells and shell detritus. It is absolutely intact.

Next to this mound in up-stream direction and partly connected with it, is an even larger conical mound, possibly 25 feet high by over 80 feet base, and of the same composition.

Still a little farther up, there is a smaller "heap," not conical; and following this were counted six heaps or mounds, one conical, the rest ridge-like or irregular. These are not exactly in a line, but as one proceeds up-stream they turn inland. These heaps are more shelly, and there are visible a good many small to moderate sized conchs, the rest being almost exclusively oyster shells, with more or less soil. Like the conical mounds, they are entirely untouched by the hand of the explorer.

This group of mounds and heaps is so beautifully situated and is in itself so characteristic, that it would seem admirably fit for a little *national reservation*. Besides which it ought to be duly explored, for though there could hardly be expected any archeological riches in a moderate sized inland settlement of this nature, there may be a good many skeletons.

Above this site it is difficult if not impossible to penetrate the river with even a small launch, and we had to return. But from information obtained from those who have trapped over this region it appears that about three miles above the site just described, on the northern bank of the same branch and not far from the bank, there is a solitary low "dirt" mound; and that about a mile above this and at some distance from the southern bank of the stream there is some "high ground" of Indian origin. It is said that the last-named "high ground" can be seen from afar and that a small "creek" runs right to it.

The exploration of the Whitney River was the brightest spot of the whole journey.

Buttonwood Key: The Buttonwood Key is situated on the "Buttonwood Bay" off the mouth of the Whitney River, and about 9 miles S. E. of the hamlet of Marco. The Key is thickly overgrown with mangrove and other vegetation, which made even a superficial survey of the place difficult. It was seen, however, that the Indian remains here are very extensive and that they consist of shell heaps and ridges, the majority of which served undoubtedly for elevated platforms for habitations. There are also smaller heaps, and one particularly large one, in which the proportion of muck and sand seems to be much greater than in others.

There are no real conical mounds, so far as it was possible to ascertain, and there were no surface indications of burials.

Shell Key: The Shell Key is located on "Shell Heap Bay," further below the mouth of the Whitney River, about 10 miles from Marco and 5 miles due east of Cape Romaine.

It was surveyed so far as the jungle and myriads of mosquitoes would permit. Part of it had at one time been cultivated. It is covered with extensive shell heaps, ridges and platforms, built up mainly of oyster shells with a smaller proportion of conchs and few clams. The heaps, etc., are generally connected and resemble much those on the not far distant Buttonwood Key. No isolated conical mounds were detected.

A good survey of the place would probably prove instructive; but the site would first have to be well cleared of vegetation.

Dismal Key: Dismal Key lies something over 13 miles S. E. of Cushing's Point on Key Marco. It has been visited by Clarence B. Moore, though he makes but a brief mention of this occasion and gives no description (p. 18, 13). About 60 acres of ground on this Key, according to the estimate of the present owner, are covered with Indian shell ridges, accumulations and mounds. A large part of this high ground is now cultivated and known, after the present owner, as Gandeese's or simply Deese's Place. It is plainly a site of a large aboriginal settlement. The ridges and heaps, as far as they could be examined, were seen to be built of oysters, with many conchs, few clam shells, some turtle shells, fish and animal bones. In one of the largest ridges, to the east of the house, two moderate-sized pits have been dug in from the side, possibly by Mr. Moore's men; they show the ridge to be composed almost exclusively of tightly packed shells and so far as archeological specimens are concerned the excavation must have been quite unproductive.

According to the present inhabitants on the Key, who however have been there only a short time, no human skeletons have yet been discovered on the place; but occasionally they find "relics" and fragments of pottery.

The site surely deserves a mapping and closer attention.

Pumpkin Key: The Pumpkin Key is situated on Pumpkin Key River—which resembles the Whitney—about 4 miles east from Deese's Place. It is located on the right bank of the river and an old abandoned house shows that the place was not long ago inhabited by a white settler; the property now belongs to Mr. Barfield, of Caximbas. The house and the place have a bad reputation for rattlesnakes, which seem to be more numerous on certain of these islands than on others.

The site is covered with extensive shell heaps, some in the nature of mounds, others in the form of ridges, and still others in that of elevated platforms. These remains cover many acres of ground, and sufficient muck has been mingled with the shells to permit of cultivation. Some of the heaps and ridges are, however, much more shelly than others. The rank vegetation and my guide's apprehension of the rattlers made a good survey of the place quite impossible; but, like the Dismal Key, it would seem to deserve closer attention.

Gomez Key: In proceeding southward and southwestward, we passed at some distance the Gomez Key, so named after a pirate, on which there are said to be some "high land" and shell heaps. It was planned to visit this key on the return journey, which, however, proved impracticable. Mr. Moore mentions (p. 6) that there are extensive shell deposits partly surrounding a basin that fills with the rising tide.

The Fakahatchee, Thompson and Ellis Places: Our route followed towards the Fakahatchee (or "Fikahatchee") Island and River (noted briefly by Mr. Moore, pp. 8, 12, 13). On the island we stopped at "Joe Thompson's Place," which was found to be another old, extensive Indian site with shell heaps, shell-muck-and-sand mounds, and other accumulations. A good-sized and rather steep conical mound, perhaps 20 feet high, is located near the house and digging in it by the settlers is said to have resulted in the discovery of human bones.

A little farther on and facing a fine bay is the pleasant home of Mr. J. B. Ellis. About 150 yards east of the Ellis house is an isolated, good-sized ridge constructed almost exclusively of oyster shells. It is about 200 feet long and 80 feet broad, by 12 to 15 feet high. The surface of this ridge was once cultivated and plowed over, which work, however, yielded so far as remembered no bones or other specimens. This mound is of very regular outline and has not as yet been dug into by any explorer.

Across the Bay from the Ellis place, on a point between the Fakahatchee and East Rivers, is the Down's Place, where a stop was made over night. The point shows but slight traces of Indians. About four miles up the Fakahatchee River there is, however, reported a shell-and-soil mound.

Ferguson River: A few miles S. E. of Down's Place is the small Ferguson River, and a short distance up this stream is reported a fair sized shell-and-soil mound, with some shell heaps.

To the west (or slightly N. W.) of the Ferguson River is *Russels Island,* on which, according to Mr. Moore (p. 9, 12, 13), and also the writer's informants, there are extensive shell heaps and mounds; and between Russels Island and Tiger Key other shell heaps are said to exist on a key, the name of which, if it has any, could not be determined.

To the southwest of Ferguson River is the Sand Fly Pass, and on one of the keys in its vicinity is the so-called "Boggass Place" where a shell-and-soil mound and shell heaps are reported.

Allen's River: This river lies a short distance S. E. of the Ferguson, and is mainly notable on account of the beautiful little settlement near its mouth known as the "Everglades." It is here that the writer had the good fortune of meeting Mr. George W. Storter to whom he is indebted for much valuable information. Mr. Storter is the hotel and store-keeper of the place, an old-timer in the region and one of the best friends of the Seminole Indians, the first representatives of whom were met with at his place.

The short and picturesque Allen River is of no great importance to archeology. About 5 or 6 miles up the river from Everglades there are several low shell heaps of moderate size, which in this flat country bear the exaggerated name of "Black Hills." In visiting these inconspicuous heaps we found them quite uninteresting, but on them were three Seminole huts with an abandoned orange grove in full bearing in the vicinity, and the fruit of the latter constituted some compensation for our journey (Pl. II).

About 2½ miles S. E. of Allen's River is the *Halfway Creek,* on which, well up stream, there is reported an Indian mound said to cover about a quarter of an acre.

PLATE II. Seminole Hut, Allen's River

PLATE III. Shell Heaps on Chokaloskee Island

in all probability other channels that lead among the shell heaps. In Mr. Moore's words, the canal runs between two graded ways, which "terminate in mounds facing each other. The easternmost mound, slightly the higher, on its western side, where it rises from the canal, has a slope of 31 degrees. Its height above the level of the bottom of the canal is 18 feet 4 inches and 22 feet 4 inches above low water level."

The settlers on Chokaloskee Island in promiscuous digging have found numerous relics, and on the western side of the island, on property now belonging to Mr. C. S. Smallwood, there were plowed up in black soil human bones belonging probably to various skeletons; unfortunately these were not preserved. The site may yet some day yield something rivalling the finds at Cushing's Point.

The keys to the west and southwest of Chokaloskee Island are said to be poor in Indian remains, though they may bear some low shell heaps. To this there are, however, two exceptions. About 2½ miles N. W. of the island is the already mentioned Sand Fly Pass, with rather extensive shell deposits; and further northwest, about 1½ or 2 miles from the Gulf and on the south side of West Pass, there is reported a good sized shell mound which has not yet been examined.

Turner's River: The paucity of Indian remains to the west of Chokaloskee Island is more than compensated for by the richness of those to the east and southeast.

Directly southeast of the Island is the mouth of Turner's River, and about half a mile up the river on the southern bank there is the most noteworthy group of shell heaps and mounds to be found in the entire region. From its present inhabitants this site is known as the *"Brown's Place."* At the edge of it there is a poor frame house in which our party found the kind, numerous and at that time both mosquito and influenza-ridden family of Mr. Brown. Notwithstanding the illness, however, we

PLATE IV. Shell Heaps on Brown's Place, Turner's River

were received in a very friendly way and Mr. Brown accompanied us over the ground which in part was being cultivated, but in a larger part was overgrown by weeds or jungle.

The remarkable remains here are intact except over a part of the least important shell accumulations which have been plowed over; and they show more plainly than any other remains seen along the coast a definite system and organization. They consist essentially of a row of 7 (there may have been originally 8 or 9) low but conspicuous shell ridges of much regularity; and of two parallel rows of large, uniform, conical mounds, running in the same direction as the shell heaps, and one ending slightly beyond these, while the other continues into the inland mangrove swamp.

These various structures—and they seem fully to deserve that name—begin close to the bank of the river, and the depressions between them may have been used originally for approach by canoes.

The shell heaps are as regular as so many swells of the ocean following each other, and are constructed of the usual material, namely, oyster shells with some conchs, a few clams, bones, etc. Some muck and sand among the shells permits of cultivation.

Above and parallel with these uniform low shell ridges is the first straight row of 8 or 9 conical, muck-sand-and-shell mounds, which, so far as could be estimated, are about 12 to 15 feet high by 60 to 70 feet in diameter at base. They are isolated, *i. e.*, not connected with each other, about equal distance apart and quite uniform in character.

Above this row of mounds is a broader depression, in which there are three large and somewhat irregular shell heaps, which, however, are far from filling the space. And beyond the depression there is a second longer row of conical, isolated equidistant and very uniform mounds, extending from near the river into

Figure 1. Shell Heaps and Mounds on Brown's Place, Turner's River

the swampy woods in the distance. This wonderful row is, according to Mr. Brown, over a quarter of a mile long. The individual mounds resemble closely those of the first row, but seem to be even more regular and more nearly circular. Like the former they are built of sandy muck with some shell admixture. Regrettably the richer ground of all these mounds, of both rows, favors vegetation so much that a good photograph of them, or even a good extended survey was impossible. But their arrangement, uniformity and intactness left a deep impression.

A few relics have been accidentally discovered on this most interesting site, but no human bones were as yet found, or any rarer specimens, which has been fortunate, favoring the preservation of the works; but this immunity may not be of long duration.

The site is so characteristic, so easily approached and probably so important to science, that steps, it would seem, ought to be taken to preserve it for posterity, which could best be done by making it a national reservation. The expense of this at present would be insignificant; and little time should be lost in having it carefully surveyed, which could be done with no great cost or difficulty at a time when the mosquito pest abates in some measure.

Upper Turner's River: About 4 miles up the river from Brown's Place is a moderate sized mound, built of small shells, but mostly soil, on the south bank of the river and near its edge. Traces of Indian camping grounds it is said occur also at other spots along the lower stretches of the river.

About 6 miles from the mouth of the river and on its southern bank, there is reported a rather prominent "heap" which probably represents an Indian site.

About 7 miles from the mouth is a piece of high ground known as "Mount Pleasant." It represents accumulations of Indian origin. And about half a mile farther north, on the northern bank, there is a moderate-sized mound.

At the head of the Turner River, in Section 36, Township 52, south 30 E. (located by the Dept. Agriculture Map), or 9 miles approximately N. E. and E. of the mouth of the river, in a cypress swamp, are reported several large Indian mounds or heaps. One of these is described as a good-sized conical mound, which may possibly contain burials.

Finally, about half a mile still further up the river, which now has become a mere creek, and on its southern side, is the *McKinney's Place*, where a lot of human bones has been discovered in a small elevation. According to Mr. Ellis, the burial "mound" on McKinney's Place was only about 2½ feet high. It was composed of dirt and rotten leaves and contained many human bones. The surface of the heap was cultivated and the bones uncovered were thrown aside; but the deposit has not been exhausted.

According to Mr. Storter, there is also an Indian mound on *Robert's Creek*, about 18 miles E. of Turner's River.

Barnes River: To the southeast of Chokaloskee Bay is the Barnes River. Not far from what is regarded as the mouth of this river and about 3 miles from the Chokaloskee Island, on a nameless key, is the so-called *Lopez Place*, on which are reported about 15 acres of shell heaps and mounds. Some of the shell heaps are said to be of good size.

On the southeast extremity of the Island and about four miles from the Lopez Place there is said to be another site with shell heaps, known as the *House's Hammock*. Some bones (human?) have been here recovered.

Neither of these places could be visited.

About 6 miles up Barnes River is reported a "dirt" mound, with possibly some shells, covering one-fourth acre or more. It is located about one-half mile N. E. of the stream on the edge of the swamp.

New River: Southeast of Barnes River and running parallel
with it is the rather insignificant New River, and at the head of
this, about 2 miles from Sunday Bay, on the southern bank of
the stream and close to its bank, is mentioned a moderate-
sized Indian mound composed mostly of soil with some shells.

About 2 miles S. E. from the head of New River there is,
according to R. E. Hamilton, a large mound which he estimates
to be at least 20 feet high, with "high land" all around. The
whole is situated in a mangrove swamp with a small creek or
canal leading to it.

A short distance further south is the *Howard Wood Creek* on
which, about 4 miles due E. from House's Hammock and about
2 miles from the mouth of the creek, is reported an Indian
mound situated on the northern bank of the creek.

Chatham Bend: A prominent water course somewhat further
south is known as the Chatham Bend "River." This river and
the so-called North Pass unite at an angle and the prominent
land forming this angle is the *"Watson's Place,"* locally famous for
a number of murders which some years ago were committed on
it and in its vicinity. Mr. Moore mentions it in one of his
reports (p. 10).

The beautiful promontory is covered with Indian remains,
mainly shell and shell-and-muck heaps, which however have
been largely plowed down and are covered with cane fields and
other cultivation. The present tender of the place, Mr. Trueman
Ivey, estimates the total of ground covered here by Indian
remains at about 40 acres. Beyond the northern limit of the
now mostly formless accumulations there are still two well-
preserved, large low oval shell-soil platforms or mounds, of
unknown purpose and contents.

Miller's Point: There is no record of any human bones having
ever been discovered on Watson's Place, but a short distance

west of the place on the opposite side of the river there is a little promontory known as *Miller's Point*, and about 400 yards further down along the bank, near the mouth of a little creek, there is a low, long burial heap. It is located almost at the edge of the river and can be located without much difficulty. Its height is only about 2 feet, but it is approximately 30 feet broad and several times that in length. It is now overgrown with mangrove, but excavations here would doubtless prove fertile so far as skeletal remains are concerned. A few years ago four skulls were taken from the surface of this mound, and later on a skeleton. The writer found some human bones on the surface, but the mosquitoes and lack of all help made excavation at the time out of question.

Chevalier Place: To the south of Chatham Bend River and the Chevalier Bay, is a narrow arm of water known as the Chevalier Pass, and the land to the west of this, with an old ramshackle, abandoned house, is known as the "Chevalier Place." Most of this consists of elevated ground partly made by the Indians and partly by former white settlers from older Indian accumulations. A little over 100 yards W. of the house and just beyond the clearing there still stand 5 oblong good-sized "hills," made of oyster shell, conchs and soil. Four are intact, while the fifth shows a small excavation. It is said that a much larger mound has been distributed over the land by the white owners, but it is not known what, if anything, had been discovered in it in the way of Indian remains. Some low shell heaps are also found along the edge of the water.

Gopher Key: The name "gopher" is applied in these regions to a large land turtle. Gopher Key is about 3½ to 4 miles W. or slightly S. W. of Chevalier Place, and is so hidden that it can only be found with an experienced guide and some good fortune. The way to it leads through Chevalier Pass, over a small, rotten sulphur-smelling "pocket" to ·he right of the pass, along a long,

PLATE V. Seminoles at Chevalier Place

narrow, almost obstructed "lost" channel leading through mangrove swamps, and over two oblong shallow "bays"—a hidden little world which is a paradise of birds, fish, alligators and mosquitoes. The key can only be approached in a very light skiff. It is about 3 miles inland from the Gulf, and was originally a low inconspicuous mangrove swamp such as all those in the neighborhood.

The landing place on the key is unpretentious. It is marked by the remnants of an old blown down shack, near which there are a number of small piles of clam shells, possibly deposited there by the white settlers who once braved the locality. Somewhat further inland there is a rich abandoned grapefruit orchard and a field, and these are located on one of the most interesting and imposing groups of mounds and heaps that exist in the Ten Thousand Islands.

Among the artificial elevations the nearest is a black soil ridge or ridge-platform, perhaps 200 feet long by 100 feet in width at the broadest part, and composed of rich mucky soil. To the S. W. of this is seen a small heap exclusively of conchs. Connected with the ridge to the N. and running E. and W., is a good sized ridge of conchs, and N. of this, over a trough about 7 feet deep, is another conch ridge running parallel with the preceding and extending northward in the form of a heap-plateau. Other elevations, some regular and bluntly conical, some ridge-like, and some in the form of irregular platforms, are located in a northern and western direction. On another black soil ridge to the north were seen old ashes; and not far distant is a good sized, conical mound, about 20 feet in diameter at the base, built entirely of conchs—so far as learned a unique occurrence for such a structure on this coast. Some of the mounds of the complex are upwards of 12 feet in height and of imposing mass. The whole site looks important and surely deserves a careful survey as well as exploration. It would make, with its approaches and surroundings, an excellent mound-bird-and-virgin-nature reservation.

Across the creek to the west of Gopher Key and about 500 yards up the stream, near where two creeks meet, on the northern bank, there is an oblong good sized oyster shell and soil mound, approximately 90 feet long by 30 across and about 5 feet in height, which was reported to be a burial place. A small excavation made by someone in the past showed only shells, but it is said that some bones had been discovered.

Shell piles occur at several places along the banks on the Gopher Key, and from the western side of the island several probably partly or wholly artificial troughs or channels can be discerned which evidently served for the approach of canoes. One or two of the unnamed keys in the vicinity are said also to contain shell accumulations.

Lossman's River: Below Gopher Key no Indian remains of consequence are known until one reaches near the mouth of Lossman's River. To the N. W. of this are the so-called Wood Key and Porpoise Point where are located the Hamiltons, local fishermen. Eastward across the bay, on a key which seems to have no definite name, though sometimes referred to as St. Mary's Island, is the place of Eugene Hamilton, and on this are located Indian accumulations of considerable interest.

The last mentioned place is approached through a narrow creek about 400 to 500 yards long, and over a recently made shell path which leads to the Hamilton's house. The house itself stands on a demolished shell heap, while other shell heaps are to the right of the house at some distance. To the left of the house and about 150 feet from it, is a large black soil ridge extending for several hundred feet in the direction of the creek and curving along the bank of this. Through this ridge has been made a narrow road and some relics as well as bones were found during the excavation.

Plate VI. Mangrove Jungle on Way to Gopher's Key

The Indian-made ground here covers on the whole, according to the estimate of the owners, about 20 acres. In addition, to the N. E. of the clearing and well in the mangrove swamp, is a very large nearly circular and uniform shell and soil mound, which thus far is entirely intact and the significance and contents of which are uncertain.

On the return journey it was observed that the creek or canal leading to the place is so regular that possibly it had been modified if not made by the Indians. The hidden nature of the whole place deep in the swamps suggests strongly a fear of enemies.

This place also seems well worth a careful exploration.

Lossman's Key: Just south of Lossman's River is the so-called Lossman's Key, on the northern end of which are shell accumulations of an old Indian site. Mr. Moore says (pp. 10, 13) they consist of "large, level causeways and platforms of shell." They were not seen.

Royal Palm Hammock: About two miles up from the mouth of Lossman's River and about ¾ mile to the south of this, there is the last remarkable Indian site known to exist along the coast. It is an oasis deep in the mangrove swamps which, from some royal palms growing on it, is known as the Royal Palm Hammock. Others, however, call it Johnson's Hammock, after a settler who at one time had the hardihood to claim it. Today the place is abandoned and most difficult of approach. It is necessary to leave the launch far away in the shallow bay, and then proceed for about half a mile through a small creek or canal on a light skiff. After that the channel becomes obstructed and it is necessary to advance a long distance along an old path between the canal and an oozy, ill-ventilated, mosquito infested swamp. The writer was accompanied on this journey by Henry Shaw, a local colored trapper and hunter, but by the time the Indian ground was reached, both of us were pretty well "done up."

The swarms of mosquitoes against which no remedy or exertion seemed to avail and the poisonous air along the damp path where the sun never penetrates, were all that a strong man could bear, and by the time the launch was reached again the effects of the journey were marked, in one of us at least, by retching, headache and general depression. Under such circumstances it will be quite evident that not much exploration of the jungle of Johnson's Hammock could be attempted. There were seen there, however, some remarkably large and steep shell heaps, wonderful productions when one reflects that all the shells had to be brought there from a long distance. There are said to be about 40 acres there of artificially made Indian ground. Perhaps some day it may be possible to carry out a satisfactory survey of this locality. Its hidden nature reflects even more than that of the site on Eugene Hamilton's place the fear of the Indians for their safety; no other reason would seem to have been weighty enough to induce them to choose such a distant and pest-ridden place for the site of their village.

The only finds reported from the place were some old white man's objects, possibly of Spanish origin.

Other Indian Remains Along the Lossman's River: Besides the above there were reported to the writer the following additional aboriginal remains along the stream under consideration:

About a mile from the mouth of the river, on its southern bank, is a shell and soil mound or ridge.

About 2½ miles from the mouth of the river and on its northern bank, there are about 5 acres of shell ridges and high land made by the Indians.

About 7 miles N. E. and E. from the mouth of the river, on "Onion Key," is an Indian camp site with some shell and soil accumulations.

Finally, about 12 to 15 miles up the river, on the mainland, there is a good sized conical mound of shell and soil (another informer spoke of this mound as being on "Rocky Creek").

Lossman's River to the Southern Extremity of the Peninsula: The part of the coast south of Lossman's River is but little known. It is said to be even more swampy or difficult of approach than the region of the Ten Thousand Islands. According to unanimous reports of the local hunters and fishermen, however, it contains no Indian remains of magnitude or importance. Mr. Moore, who circumnavigated the point, found none. The only known remains to the few local men who have been over this territory are an Indian site with some accumulations N. or N. E. of the mouth of Rogers River; a small Indian site at the head of *Harney River*, about 20 miles inland; and a few isolated heaps in the vicinity of Cape Sable.

Neither Mr. Ellis nor Mr. Storter, both of whom have been through the region about White Water Bay, Cape Sable and the southern coast of the peninsula, knew there of any Indian remains worth mentioning, with the exception of a few "mounds" and an old canal on the edge of "Mud Lake" near the southern extremity of the Cape (Ellis). Possibly this is the same site which has been spoken of by another informer as consisting of some shell heaps and a black soil with fine shell mound, located on H. C. Low's place between the middle and the east promontories of the Cape. A moderate sized mound is also mentioned as existing about 2 miles N. or N. E. from the little settlement of *Flamingo*, on the southern shore of the Cape. The rest of the southern shore is said to be so low, muddy and difficult, that no settlements of Indians would have been possible.

It is quite likely, of course, that something additional in the way of Indian remains along this part of the coast may be discovered in the future, either accidentally or through exploration; but the chances of finding there any large sites that may have escaped the sharp eye and curiosity of the local hunters and fishermen, is a very small one.

The general impressions gained from the survey of the southwestern coast of Florida may be summarized by the writer as follows:

1. The coast region from Charlotte Harbor southward is, on the whole, rich in remains of Indian occupation. This is particularly true of the Ten Thousand Islands from Key Marco to the Gopher Key and of the keys along the Lossman's River. South of Lossman's River, however, aboriginal remains appear to be few in number and of little importance.

2. The remains consist of extensive shell-heaps, shell mounds, shell and muck mounds, shell and muck ground for cultivation, and canals, with inland shelters or ponds for the canoes of the Indians.

3. The shell heaps on the various sites cover from a part of an acre to upwards of fifty acres of ground, show considerable uniformity, and are generally arranged in a parallel way, which indicates a system of construction. They consist essentially of oyster shells, with a lesser proportion of conchs, a small quantity of clams, a few turtle shells with fish and animal bones, among which is a scattering of shreds of common undecorated or but slightly decorated pottery. These heaps are not simple kitchen middens, but purposely built ridges or mounds, from all available shell. They were elevated platforms, which the Indian was obliged to build before he could feel assured of the safety of his habitation from inundation during high tides or storms. They are rather sterile though not barren of remains, both cultural and skeletal; but rare individual isolated shell mounds have served for burials.

4. The constructions of soil (sandy muck) and shell-detritus (or shell in small amount) are met with in the form of ridges, but more commonly in that of conical, more or less blunt-topped mounds of good dimensions. Such mounds occur singly or in rows. Some may have served the same purpose as the shell heaps, that is, as elevated platforms for habitations, while others may have been built over burials. As yet their contents are practically unknown.

5. Low soil-and-shell heaps occur occasionally and generally contain burials; and burials are said to have also been met with in made soil which showed no mound formation.

6. Made ground for agriculture is found in some but not other localities. It consists generally of muck with shell among which conchs may be numerous, and may in a large part represent the refuse of the habitations. In it potsherds and shell implements appear to be more common than in the heaps or mounds.

7. The shell-ridge platforms for habitations were generally so constructed that between each two there was left a good-sized trough which connected with an outer common depression, the whole system in all probability serving for channels of approach by canoes to the habitations. Longer canals or canalized creeks are found in many instances to lead to the Indian site; and sometimes there may be a channel to a single mound, for the purpose possibly of facilitating the bringing in of the material from which the mound was constructed. There are also in a number of places what appear to have been—or still are—artificial ponds or small inland harbors, which would afford a good shelter for the canoes.

These canals and harbors, like the shell-heap platforms, represent it is plain no separate culture and people, but only local and necessary developments due to peculiar environmental conditions.

8. No trace whatever was met anywhere along the coast of "pile dwellings", and it would seem that Cushing in assuming that such existed at Marco may have been mistaken, though an occasional use of short posts would have been nothing to wonder at under the conditions. The Seminoles use such short posts under their huts.

9. From Key Marco south to Chatham River the Indian sites in general are exposed; but further south there is manifest a strong tendency to seclusion in the swamps, the object of which could scarcely have been other than protection. This would indicate that the tribe or tribes were in danger of attacks by other Indians.

10. The archeological remains of the region appear to connect directly with those of Charlotte Harbor, and represent according to all indications the same culture, people and period.

The only too scanty skeletal material we thus far possess of these people indicates that they were moderately oblong to short headed, medium to tall, and moderately to strongly built Indians, similar in many respects to those whose remains are found in the mounds over a large part of the western as well as the eastern coasts of the peninsula and also in the interior. It is a type which was seemingly close to that of the present Seminoles, though these cannot be identified with the remains, being relatively newcomers to Florida from further northwest.

Judging from such scant notes as have been preserved to us on the Indians of the southwestern coast of the Peninsula, the inhabitants and builders of the great shell heaps could have been no other than the "Caloosas" (or "Calusas") who gave their name to the Caloosahatchee River, the stream flowing between Lake Okechobee and Charlotte Harbor.[1]

[1] See art. Calusas, by J. Mooney, in the Handbook of American Indians, Bull. 30, Bur. Am. Ethn.; also Safford (W. E.), Indians of Paradise Key. Smithsonian Rep., 1917.

11. Finally, a remarkable fact connected with the Indian remains of the southwestern coast, notwithstanding their frequently great extent, is the general impression of relative freshness. It is evident enough that to build such great accumulations must have taken a long time, perhaps centuries; but the earmarks of any real antiquity are wanting, which is in accord with the uniformity and paucity of archeological remains on these sites, with the relatively small number of burials, with the frequent occurrence of articles of white man's introduction, and possibly also with the commonness of marks on the bones of venereal disease.

The general conclusions which would seem to be justified from the above facts, are, that the southwestern coast of Florida from Charlotte Harbor to the end of the Peninsula was peopled during late precolumbian and well into historic times by a large Indian population of homogeneous nature culturally, though possibly not somatologically, and that these people to the northward merged with the Indians who are so well represented in the secondary burials on some of the Keys and in the mounds of the St. John's River.

The remaining problems are just what became of all this population as well as of the more northern large coastal group; exactly what these groups were; and whether or not the remains of the Caloosas group may have merged with parts of the Seminole tribe. Of course we know of their struggles with the Spanish and their partial deportation; but it seems strange that such a large population, not only of the west coast but also of other parts of Florida, should have completely disappeared since the Spanish connections with the Peninsula.

FORT MYERS TO LAKE OKECHOBEE AND THE EAST COAST

The road from Fort Myers to Lake Okechobee leads over, or in the vicinity of, the Caloosahatchee River. Along this river are a number of more or less insignificant sand mounds, probably with burials.

About 8 miles N. E. of the small town of Labelle, however, there is a large sand mound, which may be seen indicated on the Agricultural map of the country. This mound has been spoken of by so many who have visited the region that the writer was anxious to see it. As so often happens, however, the reality fell considerably below the aroused expectations. Nevertheless there was found a huge heap of white sand, oval in outline, about 20 to 25 feet in height and approximately 160 yards in circumference at the base. A number of excavations have been made by local explorers in the mound, but so far as could be learned without results. The largest of these holes was, however, only about 7 to 8 feet deep and the interior of the mound has as yet been untouched. It is quite likely that it contains some burials.

Between Labelle and Lake Okechobee nothing of importance in the way of Indian remains could be learned of, and the same applies to the vicinity of the lake itself. There are traces of Indian occupation, but they are not conspicuous. The many canals which have been and are now being constructed both to the west and to the east of the lake, have as far as could be learned failed to reveal any Indian remains of consequence. Perhaps the most interesting was the discovery of an old dug-out canoe, which is now on exhibition in the garden of the lady Mayor of Moore Haven (1918).

It appears that no mounds have as yet been located either about Lake Okechobee or to the east of it. The interior of the peninsula at this latitude is, therefore, according to all indications so far, much more sterile in Indian remains of all sorts than the coast regions.

THE SEMINOLES

The Seminole Indians, now about 560 strong,[1] are scattered and roam over most of southern Florida below the latitude of Lake Okechobee. They can frequently be met with individually or in small parties among the Ten Thousand Islands. A few work occasionally for the whites, but the large majority prefer to live freely in the wilderness, moving from place to place in small groups.

As no somatic data on a full-blood Seminole have as yet been secured and the tribe is of some importance, it was the hope of the writer that he would meet a few individuals or groups along the coast and that perhaps some of these Indians might prove full-bloods and be induced to submit to a few measurements. Those contingents of the tribe which visit the eastern coast are known to contain a good deal of admixture of white as well as some negro blood; but those of the southwest coast have never been reported upon except by the local whites, who claimed that any form of miscegenation was exceedingly rare in this region.

The expectation of finding some of the natives was realized, though only in a small measure. The total seen were four young men. Two of these were found at Mr. Storter's place at Everglades and two were met accidentally—one in an old dug-out and one in a new one which he was leisurely finishing at each stop—on the shore at the abandoned Chevalier place further south. Of these four, two were mix-bloods, one very plainly so, but two seemed to be free from admixture, and one of these submitted to measurements. Two of the men were also photographed (see Pl. VII). A larger party regrettably was missed at Chatham Bend by only a few hours.

---

[1] The latest official number was 585, but recently there were a series of deaths in the tribe from influenza. On January 16th ten were reported to have thus died, but the number is probably greater.

The full-blood impress one as typical, ordinary Indians. The two seen were slightly deeper than medium brown in color, with straight black hair and the general characteristics of the oblong to slightly short-headed type of the native. The stature was moderate to fair, the body and limbs well developed. The one who submitted to measurements gave the following proportions:

```
Name—Boy Jim.
Age—Approximately 20-22.
Full-blood Seminole in appearance.
Stature.......................................................... 165    cm.
Head: Maximum length..................................... 18.4   "
      Maximum breadth.................................... 14.9   "
      Height (from line connecting floors of auditory canals to
          bregma)........................................... 13.6   "
Cephalic Index.............................................. 81.0
Cephalic module (or mean diameter)....................... 15.63 cm.
Mean Height Index (mean of length + breadth)/height ..... 77.4
Face: Height to nasion..................................... 11.9 cm.
      Height to crinion.................................... 17.7   "
      Diameter bizygomial maximum........................ 13.6   "
      Diameter frontal minimum........................... 10.0   "
      Diameter bigonial................................... 10.4   "
Facial Index, lower........................................ 67.2
Facial Index, total........................................ 76.8
Nose: Height............................................... 5.6 cm.
      Breadth............................................. 3.8   "
Nasal Index................................................ 67.9
Mouth: Breadth............................................ 5.4 cm.
Left Ear: Height.......................................... 5.8   "
          Breadth......................................... 3.4   "
Ear Index................................................. 58.6
```

All of these measurements and indices, it will be recognized, are quite common for a south eastern, medium developed, young adult or slightly subadult Indian.

PLATE VII. Seminoles near Chevalier Place

PLATE VIII. Seminoles, on Allen River

Photo given by Mr. George H. Storms

PLATE IX. Approximate General Distribution of the Rounded (red) and the Oblong (blue) Headed Types in Florida

II

THE PEOPLING AND TRIBES OF FLORIDA

WHEN Ponce de León and his companions reached Florida in 1512 or '13, they found the peninsula peopled by sedentary Indians. These were divided into several tribes speaking different dialects, if not languages, and occupying each a certain "province."

These natives, as far as recorded, gave no information as to the time or way of their coming into the peninsula, or of their blood relation to other tribes. They were found to have had some contacts with the Indians of Cuba (Fontaneda),[1] and there are archeological as well as other evidences of their contacts with the neighboring tribes of the continent.

Among themselves they lived partly in amity, partly in discord. They had numbers of more or less grouped villages along the Atlantic and the Gulf coasts, about the inland sounds and lakes, and along the rivers. Their organization and culture were found to be in the main like those of the southern tribes in general. They lived on molluscs, fish, game, roots, wild fruit with vegetables raised in gardens or small fields. They were largely a canoe people, and the men were reputed as fighters. Living predominantly on the low, swampy, mangrove- and insect-plagued keys and coasts, that were further liable to inundation during storms, they constructed extensive shell-heaps that would serve as safe, dry and clean platforms for their habitations. They also constructed canals and sheltered lagoons

---

[1] Fontaneda (H. de Escalante). Memoria de las cosas y costa y Indios de la Florida. (Documentos inéditos, v, 532–546, Madrid, 1866. *Same* in Smith (B.). Letter of Hernando de Soto and Memoir of H. de E. Fontaneda, Washington, 1854. *Same* Fr. trans. in Terneaux-Compans, Voyages, xx, 9–42, Paris, 1841.)

for their canoes, brought where necessary the shell detritus and muck for their gardens, and built sand and shell mounds for burials and other purposes.

According to Brinton[1] there were six main districts and tribes. Commencing at the south, the extremity of the peninsula was "divided into two independent provinces, one called Tegesta on the shores of the Atlantic, the other and most important on the west or Gulf coast possessed by the Caloosa Tribe." According to Fontaneda the latter province extended along the west coast from Tampa Bay southward and about Lake Okechobee. The Province of Tegesta embraced a string of villages of fishermen stretching from Cape Cañaveral to the southern extremity of the peninsula. A third province was situated to the "north of the province of Callos, throughout the country around the Hillsboro River, and from it probably to the Withlacoochee, and easterly to the Ocklawaha"; a fourth included the region of the present Marion and Alachua Counties; a fifth comprised the lands drained by the St. John's River; and a sixth extended from the mouth of the St. John's River northward along the coast as far as the Savannah.

Of the Calusa tribe there is some further information[2] which is thus resumed by James Mooney: This "important tribe of Florida was formerly holding the southwest coast from about Tampa Bay to Cape Sable and Cape Florida, together with all the outlying keys, and extending inland to Lake Okechobee. They claimed more or less authority also over the tribes of the east coast north to about Cape Cañaveral.

"Their history begins in 1513, when, with a fleet of eighty canoes, they boldly attacked Ponce de León who was about to land on their coast, and after an all-day fight compelled him to

---

[1] Brinton (Daniel G.). Notes on the Floridian Peninsula, its Literary History, Indian Tribes and Antiquities. 12mo, Philadelphia, 1859, 112.
[2] Calusa. *Handb. Am. Indians*, Bull. xxx, Bur. Am. Ethnol., Pt. 1, 195–196.

withdraw. Two centuries later they were regarded as veritable pirates. From one of their villages the modern Tampa takes its name. Another, Muspa, existed up to about 1750. About the year 1600 they carried on a regular trade by canoe with Havana. . . . By the constant invasion of the Creeks and other Indian allies of the English in the XVIII century they were at last driven from the mainland and forced to take refuge on the keys, particularly Key West, Key Vaccas and the Matacumbe Keys. Romans states that in 1763, on the transfer of Florida from Spain to England, the last remnant of the tribe numbering then 80 families, or perhaps 350 souls, was removed to Havana. This, however, is only partially correct, as a considerable band under the name of Muspa Indians, or simply Spanish Indians, maintained their distinct existence and language in their ancient territory up to the close of the second Seminole war. Nothing definite is known of the linguistic affinity of the Calusa, or their immediate neighbors"; though Brinton and Cushing were inclined to class the dialects of the west coast with the Muskhogean.[1]

As to the more northern tribes, known from their language collectively as Timucua, we have the following further information summarized also by James Mooney:[2] They were "a group of cognate tribes formerly occupying the greater part of North Florida, extending along the east coast from about lat. 28°, below Cape Cañaveral, to above the mouth of St. John's River, and along the west coast probably from Tampa Bay northward to about Ocilla River where they met the Appalachee of Muskhogean stock. The Hichiti and Yamasee, also Muskhogean, appear to have occupied their north frontier nearly on the present state boundary; but the Timucua held both banks of St.

[1] Cushing (Frank Hamilton). Exploration of Ancient Key-Dweller Remains on the Gulf Coast of Florida. *Proc. Am. Philos. Soc.*, 1897, xxxv, 105 *et seq.*
[2] Timucuan Family. *Handb. Am. Indians*, Bull. 30, Bur. Am. Ethnol., Pt. 2, 752–754.

Mary's River and Cumberland Island. South of lat. 28° the west coast was held by the Calusa and the east coast by the Ais and Tequesta." Other Timucua tribes were Saturiba on the lower St. John; Yustaga, or Hostaqua about the upper Suwanee; Potano west of St. John's River between the heads of the Withlacoochee and Suwanee; Tocobaga between Withlacoochee River and Tampa Bay; Mayaca on the northeast coast; and Marracou, 40 leagues from the mouth of St. John's River.

"The history of the Timucuan tribes begins with the landing of Ponce de Leòn near the site of the present St. Augustine in 1513. In 1528 Narvaez led his small army from Tampa Bay northward to explore the country of the Apalachee and beyond. In 1539 de Soto went over nearly the same route, his historians mentioning some twenty tribal or local names within the region, including Yustage and Potano. In 1562–64 the French Huguenots under Ribault and Laudonnière attempted settlements at the mouth of St. John's River, explored the middle course of the stream and the adjacent interior and became acquainted with the tribes of Saturiba (Satouiroua) and Timucua (Thimagoa), as well as the Potano (Potanou) and Yustage (Hostaqua), already visited by De Soto. In 1565 the Spaniards under Menendez destroyed the French posts, killing all their defenders; they then founded St. Augustine and began the permanent colonization of the country. Within a few years garrisons were established and missions founded." In the course of time, "the Timucuan tribes in general, particularly along the east coast, accepted Christianity and civilization and became the allies of the Spaniards. . . . About 1703, began the series of invasions by the English of Carolina and their savage Indian allies, Creek, Catawba and Yuchi, by which the missions were destroyed, hundreds of men, women and children carried off into slavery, while the remnant took refuge close under the walls of St. Augustine. The prosperous Apalachee missions shared the same fate. With the decline of the Spanish power and the incessant inroads of the Creeks and Seminoles, the native Indians rapidly dwindled until on the transfer of the territory to the United States, 1821, only a handful remained, and these apparently belonging mostly to the uncivilized tribes of the southern end. It is possible that the remnant of the mission tribes had been later shipped to Cuba by the Spaniards, as had been the case with the Calusa in 1763."

As to the incursions and settlement in Florida of the more northern tribes, we have the following additional helpful account by Brinton:[1]

"About the close of the seventeenth century, when the tribes who originally possessed the peninsula had become dismembered and reduced by prolonged conflicts with the whites, and between themselves, various bands from the more Northern regions, driven from their ancestral home partly by the English and partly by a spirit of restlessness, sought to fix their habitations in various parts of Florida.

"The earliest of these were the Savannahs or Yemassees (Yammassees, Jamasees, Eamuses), a branch of the Muskogeh or Creek nation, who originally inhabited the shores of the Savannah River and the low country of Carolina. Here they generally maintained friendly relations with the Spanish, who at one period established missions among them, until the arrival of the English. These purchased their land, won their friendship, and embittered them against their former friends. As the colony extended, they gradually migrated southward, obtaining a home by wresting from their red and white possessors the islands and mainland along the coast of Georgia and Florida. The most disastrous of these inroads was in 1686, when they

---

[1] Notes on the Floridian Peninsula, etc., 139 *et seq.* In these connections see also the most recent and thorough work on the "Early History of the Creek Indians and their Neighbours," by John R. Swanton, *Bull. 73*, Bur. Am. Ethnol., Wash., 1922.

drove the Spanish colonists from all the islands north of the St. John's, and laid waste the missions and plantations that had been commenced upon them. Subsequently, spreading over the savannas of Alachua and the fertile plains of Middle Florida, they conjoined with the fragments of older nations to form separate tribes, as the Chias, Canaake, Tomocos or Atimucas, and others. Of these, the last mentioned were the most important. They dwelt between the St. John's and the Suwannee, and possessed the towns of Jurlo Noca, Alachua, Nuvoalla, and others. At the devastation of their settlements by the English and Creeks in 1704 and 1706, they removed to the shores of Musquito Lagoon, 65 miles south of St. Augustine, where they had a village, long known as the Pueblo de Atimucas.

"A portion of the tribe remained in Carolina, dwelling on Port Royal Island, whence they made frequent attacks on the Christian Indians of Florida, carrying them into captivity, and selling them to the English. In April, 1715, however, instigated as was supposed by the Spanish, they made a sudden attack on the neighboring settlements, but were repulsed and driven from the country." They hastened to St. Augustine, "where they were given a spot of ground within a mile of the city. Here they resided till the attack of Colonel Palmer in 1727, who burnt their village and destroyed most of its inhabitants. Some, however, escaped, and to the number of twenty men, lived in St. Augustine about the middle of the century. Finally, this last miserable remnant was enslaved by the Seminoles, and sunk in the Ocklawaha branch of that tribe.

"Originating from near the same spot as the Yemassees were the Uchees. When first encountered by the whites, they possessed the country on the Carolina side of the Savannah River for more than 150 miles commencing 60 miles from its mouth, and, consequently, just west of the Yemassees. Closely associated with them there were the Palachoclas or Apalachicolos.

About the year 1716, nearly all the latter, together with a portion of the Uchees, removed to the south under the guidance of Cherokee Leechee, their chief, and located on the banks of the stream called by the English the Flint River, but which subsequently received the name of Apalachicola.

"The rest of the Uchees clung tenaciously to their ancestral seats in spite of the threats and persuasion of the English, till after the middle of the century, when a second and complete migration took place. Instead of joining their kinsmen, however, they kept more to the east, occupying sites first on the headwaters of the Altamaha, then on the Santilla (St. Tillis), St. Mary's, and St. John's, where we hear of them as early as 1786. At the cession of the United States (1821), they had a village 10 miles south of Volusia, near Spring Gardens. At this period, though intermarrying with their neighbors, they still maintained their identity, and when, at the close of the Seminole war in 1845, 250 Indians embarked at Tampa for New Orleans and the West it is said a number of them belonged to this tribe, and probably constituted the last of the race.

"While these movements were taking place from the north toward the south, there were also others in a contrary direction. One of the principal of these occurred while Francisco de la Guerra was Governor-General of Florida (1684–1690), in consequence of an attempt made by Don Juan Marquez to remove the natives to the West India islands and enslave them. We have no certain knowledge how extensive it was, though it seems to have left quite a number of missions deserted.

"What has excited more general attention is the tradition of the Shawnees (Shawanees, Sawannees, Shawanos), that they originally came from the Suwannee River in Florida, whose name has been said to be 'a corruption of Shawanese,' and that they were driven thence by the Cherokees. That such was the origin of the name is quite false, as its present appellation is merely a corruption of the Spanish San Juan, the river having been called the Little San Juan, in contradistinction to the St. John's (el rio de San Juan), on the eastern coast. Nor did they ever live in this region, but were scions of the Savannah stem of the Creeks, accolents of the river of that name, and consequently were kinsmen of the Yemassees.

"The Seminoles, the Creek nation, so called, says Adair, from the number of streams that intersected the lowlands they inhabited, more properly Muskogeh (corrupted into Muscows), sometimes Western Indians, as they were supposed to have come later than the Uchees, and on the early maps Cowetas (Couitias), and Allibamons from their chief towns, was the last of those waves of migration which poured across the Mississippi for several centuries prior to Columbus. Their hunting grounds at one period embraced a vast extent of country reaching from the Atlantic coast almost to the Mississippi. After the settlement of the English among them, they diminished very rapidly from various causes, principally wars and ravages of the smallpox, till about 1740 the whole number of their warriors did not exceed 1500. The majority of these belonged to that branch of the nation, called from its more southern position the Lower Creeks, of mongrel origin, made up of the fragments of numerous reduced and broken tribes, dwelling north and northwest of the Floridian peninsula.

"When Governor Moore of South Carolina made his attack on St. Augustine, he included in his complement a considerable band of this nation. After he had been repulsed they kept possession of all the land north of the St. John's, and, uniting with certain negros from the English and Spanish colonies, formed the nucleus of the nation, subsequently called Ishti semoli, wild men, corrupted into Seminolies and Seminoles, who subsequently possessed themselves of the whole peninsula and still remain there. Others were introduced by the English in their subsequent invasions, by Governor Moore, by Col. Palmer, and by General Oglethorpe. As early as 1732, they had founded the town of Coweta on the Flint River, and laid claim to all the country from there to St. Augustine. They soon began to make incursions independent of the whites, as that led by Toonahowi in 1741, as that which in 1750, under the guidance of Secoffee, forsook the banks of the Apalachicola, and settled the fertile savannas of Salachua, and as the band that in 1808 followed Micco Hadjo to the vicinity of Tallahassie. They divided themselves into seven independent bands, the Latchivue or Latchione, inhabiting the level banks of the St. John's, and the sand hills to the west, near the ancient fort Poppa (San Francisco de Pappa), opposite Picolati, the Oklevuaha, or Oklewaha on the river that bears their name, the Chokechatti, the Pyaklekaha, the Talehouyana or Fatehennyaha, the Topkelake, and a seventh, whose name I cannot find.

"They usually interred the dead, and carefully concealed the grave for fear it should be plundered and desecrated by enemies, though at other times, as after battle, they piled the slain indiscriminately together, and heaped over them a mound of earth.

"Ever since the first settlement of these Indians in Florida they have been engaged in a strife with the whites."

Since the "second Seminole war" (1836–42) a remnant of the tribe, now between five and six hundred strong, is settled and roams over the wild region of the Everglades and the Ten Thousand Islands.

NUMBERS; ANTIQUITY

After everything that has been written on the Florida Indians is perused there remain two strong outstanding impressions. One is how very little is known about them; and the other is how completely they have vanished. Considering the size of the territory there is no other like example in both respects on the north American continent, and the circumstance raises with a double interest the question as to the numbers of the Florida Indians before the conquest. On this there are two angles of evidence, one the old records, and the other the material remains left by the tribes.

Numbers.—Fontaneda, speaking of the Calusa in about 1570, gives them 50 villages of 30 to 40 persons each, or the total of between 1500 and 2000 persons, which in view of our present knowledge of their remains seems too low. Of the Indians further north there are no collective estimates, but the cacique Vitachuco was reported to have opposed De Soto with thousands of warriors, and there are other instances of high numerical estimates of these natives by the early Spaniards. In the easily shared opinion of Brinton,[1] however, we must regard such estimates as "the hyperbole of men describing an unknown and strange land, supposed to abound in marvels of every description. The natural laws that regulate the increase of all hunting tribes, the analogy of other nations of equal civilization, the nature of the country, and lastly, the adverse testimony of these same writers, forbid us to entertain any other supposition."

Brinton ventures an estimate of his own on this occasion, and he may have erred somewhat in the other direction. In his opinion, "Including men, women and children, the aboriginal population of the whole peninsula probably but little exceeded at any one time 10,000 souls"; which for the maximum of the Floridian native population about the time of discovery is probably too low. The natives were much more than mere hunting tribes, but it remains certain that the estimates of the Spaniards, as on so many other occasions, were exaggerations. Much larger numbers could not possibly have melted away so completely between the sixteenth and the beginning of the nineteenth century as have the Floridians, of whom since about

---

[1] Brinton (Daniel G.). Floridian Peninsula, etc., 111, 112.

1820 not a known living trace remains; they have not even left any mixed population, though some traces of their blood are probably coursing in the veins of the Seminoles who have roamed since over the southern parts of the peninsula.

The bearing of the evidence of the material remains of the Florida natives as to the numerical strength of the population will, when once exact data become more available, be very substantial. As it is, all the needed facts are not yet at the student's disposal—still enough is known to afford some indications.

The material remains of the old native Floridian population consist essentially of shell-heaps and mounds. Due to the peculiar nature of conditions on the peninsula, these heaps and mounds constitute an index of expended labor, of the number and extent of the settlements, and of the approximate numbers of burials. All this is complicated by the as yet uncertain time element, but the task is seemingly not as complex as in some other regions. It is improbable that all the sites were occupied or peopled to the maximum at the time of discovery, and the accumulation of burials has doubtless taken many generations; yet plainly these remains enclose a story which, when once properly interpreted, will be of great help to the student seeking a solution of the question of the numbers of the Floridian population.

The shell-heaps, mounds, canals and other works left by these Indians are many in number. They are so numerous in some regions and so extensive collectively and even individually, that at first sight they forcibly suggest many people as well as long habitation. But a careful examination does not sustain the impression of any great numbers, except perhaps in a few localities. In a majority of cases the settlement, like its site and resources, was, it is plainly seen, small to moderate, and there were not many to which one could attribute at any one time over one hundred families. And the evidence of the burial mounds is even more convincing—they are not enough in number nor abundant enough in contents to denote more than a moderate population. Possibly twice to three times the estimate of Brinton, or say twenty-five to thirty thousand, would be a fair approximation of the total number of the Florida Indians at the time of discovery.

Antiquity.—The antiquity of man in Florida has already been the subject of many discussions and controversies,[1] and the end of these may not be expected so long, on one hand, as the peninsula will continue to yield human bones that have become petrified or been found in association with those of extinct animals, and so long, on the other, as there will be men credulous or uncritical enough to accept these as proofs of man's antiquity in that region. Both of which are indefinite propositions. The peninsula is so rich in fossils of extinct species that an occasional association with human burials or bones is unavoidable, and the land presents such peculiar and active mineralogical conditions that petrifaction of bones or their inclusion in rock is frequently rapid and gives results that elsewhere would deserve the most earnest attention. The difficulty in Florida, in fact, is not to find a more or less "fossilized" human bone, but to find one a few centuries old that would not be more or less mineralized, or embedded into a more or less consolidated material. That these facts have been and will probably be again and again misinterpreted by men, even by scientific men who in their own lines are far more careful and critical, cannot but be expected.

As a matter of fact we have no human remains from Florida, or from any other part of the North or South American continent, that could conscientiously be accepted as representing man of

---

[1] See Hrdlička (A.). "The Fossil Man of Western Florida" in "Skeletal Remains Suggesting or Attributed to Early Man in North America." *Bull. 33*, Bur. Am. Ethnol., Washington, 1907, 53–66; and "The 'Fossil' Man of Vero, Florida," in "Recent Discoveries Attributed to Early Man in America," *Bull. 66*, Bur. Am. Ethnol., Washington, 1918, 23–65.

antiquity beyond a few thousand years at most, and of other than the ordinary Indian type; nor are there apparent any indications that anything much older may in these parts of the world be yet discovered.

In many parts of Florida, along the coast, in proximity with the big inland rivers, and especially on the western keys, there are great shell heaps. But the shell heaps are seen to have been made of all the available shells, not only the house refuse, and so the problem is merely how long it would take, with the well-known industry of the Indian women and under the spur of conditions, to bring such impressive accumulations into existence. As to the contents, the shells are all recent, and often fresh enough inside of the heap to preserve more or less of their delicate colors. There is no trace of any discontinuity or superposition. The work materials, the archeology, are uniform in the essentials, and the culture except in local developments or adaptations and possibly a few introductions from the south, corresponds to that of the more northern tribes at the time of discovery.

The burial mounds speak even more plainly. In the first place a large proportion of the hitherto explored mounds, on the west coast evidently the majority, have been found to contain articles of white man's introduction, which may in general be taken as a safe indication that they were not finished or even constructed until after the beginning of the sixteenth century. And the remaining mounds with their burials are not enough in number to denote more than a moderate period of occupation. A few centuries before the coming of the whites would suffice.

At this point the question obtrudes itself whether the mound-building Indians of the peninsula may not have been preceded by people who did not build mounds, and buried in the ground. There is no archeological evidence of such an occupation. Inland and perhaps in favorable spots even along the coasts occasional isolated burials are found in the ground. But the examination of the remains has shown invariably either some unsolvable but relatively trivial ambiguity, or just the ordinary Indian. On the keys and most of the coast, the swamps, mangroves and other conditions would at any time have made the digging of a grave exceedingly difficult if not impossible, and therefore the burial mounds here may safely be regarded as an index of the population, the more so as not a few of them contain secondary mass burials of remains of bodies that were brought to the mound from wherever they may have lain temporarily. All that may be said in this connection, therefore, is that if any people have preceded the mound and shell-heap population in Florida, they must have been few in numbers, of similar culture and of Indian derivation.

So far as the *peopling* of Florida is concerned there appears to be no alternative therefore to the conclusion that it was a relatively late event in the peopling of the continent, and one without much consequence. That before being peopled, parts of the peninsula may have been the hunting ground of parties of aborigines from farther north is quite possible. The lateness of actual peopling of the land may well have been due to its plagues of mosquitoes, other insects and reptiles, with its meagre fitness for agriculture, and under- rather than over-population of the neighboring mainland regions. Whence the eventual population was derived will be shown by the comparison of its skeletal remains, though many other considerations point north and northwest. It never reached great numerical, cultural or political importance. Due to war, disease and deportation it has long since completely disappeared, though its traces may yet be discoverable among the Everglade Seminoles.

PHYSICAL CHARACTERISTICS

As to the physical characteristics of the Florida population at the advent of the whites, there are only a small number of references, and these are of little if any value. Cabeza de Vaca,[1] writing of his trip to Florida with Narvaez in 1527, reports the Floridians to be "wonderfully well built, spare, very strong and very swift," adding that "being so tall and going about nude they look like giants from a distance." Lucas Vasquez de Ayllon and Le Moyne each speak of having seen giant-like caciques,[2] the former adding, for good measure, that in the case of his cacique the giantism had been produced artificially by the Indians. These and similar reports on the Muskhogees, the Indians of South Carolina, etc., influenced more than one subsequent author, among whom no less keen a critic than Brinton, who in his "Floridian Peninsula" (p. 171), speaking of skeletons from a mound on Long Key, Sarasota Bay, reports of having been assured "by an intelligent gentleman of Manatee" that some of these "were of astonishing size and must have belonged to men 7 or 8 feet in height"; which statement, Brinton adds, "is not so incredible as it may appear at first sight," quoting some other reports of that nature from other parts of the continent. And the "giant" and "eight-foot" skeleton is to this day the almost stereotyped feature of many an amateur report of a find of skeletal remains from Florida as well as other parts of the country. All these reports on the Floridians as well as other Indians, it may be said once for all, are exaggerations.

There are in addition to the above a few references to the color and general appearance of the people, from which little can be made out except that the color was darker in the south.

PHYSICAL ANTHROPOLOGY

The above few references make it plain that scientific knowledge of the physical characteristics of the Floridian natives has

---

[1] Naufragios de Alvar Nuñez Cabeza de Vaca, etc., Historiadores primitivos de Indias, Madrid, 1858, 1, 517.

[2] See Ecker (A.). *Arch. f. Anthrop.*, 1877, x, 112 et seq.

been but little benefited by travellers and historians; and as will
be seen shortly, it has not been advanced much beyond that by
trained observers.   This notwithstanding the fact that so many
burial mounds and shell-heaps—which latter also occasionally
contain burials—are disseminated over the peninsula, and that
most of these perhaps have already been explored or at least dug
into by amateur collectors.   In addition; a series of the shell
heaps have been partly or completely removed for road-making,
revealing now and then human skeletons, while other mounds
have been partly washed away in storms or ploughed over,
disclosing burials.   All this has resulted in the discovery of very
considerable quantities of skeletal remains of the Indians who
once peopled the peninsula, but due in part to the mostly poor
state of preservation of these remains, but mainly to lack of
sufficient interest in the bones or a lack of knowledge as to what
to do with these, the larger number by far of such remains have
been lost or have reached our collections in a more or less frag-
mentary condition.   Added to this may be the fact that the
southern portion of the peninsula is still but thinly peopled and
presents many natural obstacles to exploration, due to which it
has received much less attention by archeologists than parts
further north and remains almost unrepresented in our collections
so far as skeletal material is concerned.

The total number of better preserved Florida crania now in
scientific collections may be estimated at a little over 300,
besides which there are, particularly in the U. S. National
Museum, numerous single parts of skeleton and many fragments.
Of this material a small series is in Germany, the rest being
preserved in Washington, Philadelphia, Boston and New York.
These remains have been partly studied and reported upon as
follows:

In 1871, in the Fourth Annual Report of the Peabody
Museum (pp. 12, 13–18), Jeffries Wyman briefly describes and

gives essential measurements of 18 more or less imperfect skulls from a small sand mound a few miles from Cedar Keys, in the northern part of the west coast of the peninsula. Dr. Wyman's brief account of these specimens reads:

"The burials were all of the rudest kind. No indications of approximate age of the mound were found, nor could information with regard to its history be obtained. The trees growing upon the mound were none of them more than half a century old. The bones were all greatly decayed by the destruction of the organic matter, and it was only with the greatest care that they could be removed without injury or even complete destruction. When dried they acquired greater firmness, but could only be preserved and handled after being immersed in gelatine.

"The capacity of the skulls is 1375 cc., or nearly 84 cubic inches, and is greater than that of the mound crania. The foramen magnum is quite far back, its index being .374, very nearly the same as that of the crania just referred to, but there are no signs whatever of distortion. They are remarkable for massiveness and thickness. The average thickness through the parietal bones in eight of them amounting to 10.5 mm. or 0.42 inch, or almost double the usual thickness, and in this respect they contrast very strikingly with skulls from the mounds, as they also do in the general roughness of the surfaces for muscular attachments on the hinder part of the head.

"The skulls are quite heavy, but in consequence of the destruction of the bones of the face in most of them, the whole weight could be had in a single instance only. This happens to be the heaviest of the series, weighing 995 grams, and notwithstanding the loss of its organic matter is heavier than any of the 300 skulls of various races in our collection."

In 1875 Jeffries Wyman, in his larger report on the "Fresh Water Shell Mounds of the St. John's River, Florida,"[1] gives

---

[1] *Fourth Memoir*, Peabody Acad. Sc., 8vo., Salem, Mass., 1875.

CRANIA FROM CEDAR KEYES, FLORIDA, REPORTED BY JEFFRIES WYMAN*

	Mean	Minimum	Maximum
Length of Occipital	(15) 11.9	10.8	14.1
Length of Parietal	(15) 12.1	10.8	14.0
Length of Frontal	(15) 12.6	11.6	13.5
Longitudinal Arch	(14) 37.–	34.6	39.5
Occipital Arch	(16) 23.5	21.7	24.7
Parietal Arch	(16) 34.0	30.7	36.4
Frontal Arch	(17) 30.2	29.0	35.8
Index of Foramen Magnum	37.4	34.3	40.0
Index of Height	(11) 77.7	73.5	85.0
Index of Breadth	(16) 83.0	78.3	88.8
Breadth of Frontal	(17) 9.85	9.3	10.8
Height	(11) 13.56	12.5	14.2
Breadth	(18) 14.5	13.7	15.7
Length	(16) 17.35	16.5	18.9
Circumference	(16) 50.5	48.0	54.0
Capacity	(7)** 1376	1210	1570

* No separation has been made of deformed specimens.
** These numbers show the number of crania subjected to the measurement indicated in the respective columns.

brief notes on various skeletal remains from the mounds along the river, including a description, with measurements, of a skull from the Osceola Mound. As this skull was damaged through an injury the measurements are of no value. Special attention is given to the flattening of the tibia (platycnemy).

In 1878 brief observations with the principal measurements on 20 skulls and a few other parts of the skelton, derived from the same mound at Cedar Keys from which came Wyman's material, were published by Ecker.[1] Ecker notes that a number of the specimens show artificial deformation, but mistakes this for the "macrocephalic" or Aymara type. He further calls attention to the thickness of some of the skulls and also to their height. The cephalic index ranges from 74.7 to 89.4, the majority (12) being above 80; but no allowance or elimination has been made for or on account of the deformation. Influenced by the apparent size of the skulls together with their thickness, strong muscular attachments and size of the lower jaw, Ecker regrettably adheres to the fallacy that the people whom these remains represent must have been of "Herculean" proportions, in support of which he cites Brinton and other authors. On this basis he also concludes that the people to whom these remains belonged were in all probability the same that were met in these localities by the first whites. And he falls into another error in considering these people as different from a "much older" population that constructed the shell heaps. The article is a good example of how dangerous it is even for men of calibre to generalize from insufficient material and to take for facts the exaggerations of "reliable persons", with the errors of preceding authors.

In 1880 George A. Otis in his "List of the Specimens in the Anatomical Section of the United States Army Medical Museum"

[1] Ecker (A.). Zur Kenntniss des Körperbaues früherer Einwohner der Halbinsel Florida. *Arch. f. Anthrop.*. 1878, x, 101–114, 3 pl.

gives a few measurements on a series of Florida skulls; but as the measurements are known to have been taken under circumstances which make it impossible to give them full reliance, the data are of but little account. Since then these skulls, originally from the Smithsonian Institution, have been retransferred to the U. S. National Museum and form part of the material made use of for the report of the present writer.

In 1896, Harrison Allen published a memoir on "Crania from the Mounds of the St. John's River, Florida."[1] Regrettably the report is limited to 5 skulls, the only ones "found in sufficiently good condition to describe" out of 33 crania "collected by Mr. Clarence B. Moore from prehistoric Indian graves in Florida"; the bulk of the memoir being given to measurements and desscriptions of skulls from other parts of the north American continent. Also some of the measurements and parts of the nomenclature, taken after Meigs, are not those in general use today, which makes them somewhat difficult to follow. But the engravings are excellent, following in size and style those of Morton's "Crania Americana." For comparison, Allen gives a series of measurements, the first ever published, on skulls of Seminoles, besides those on crania of other Indians, and gives original studies on teeth, jaws, the malar bone, the nasal index and other particulars.

As all the crania from Florida in the collections of the Academy of Natural Sciences in Philadelphia, including those seen by Harrison Allen, have been re-examined and measured by the writer, there is no use of quoting Allen's data, and he has formulated no concise deductions. Accepting the views of Bartram and Jones[2] that "at least some of the Indians of Florida,

---

[1] *J. Ac. Nat. Sc.*, Philadelphia, 4°, 367–448, pl. xlix–lxx.

[2] Bartram (Wm.). Travels through North and South Carolina, Georgia, etc., Philadelphia, 1791, London, 1792. Jones (Chas. C., Jr.). Antiquities of the Southern Indians, particularly of the Georgia tribes, New York, 1873.

after the settlement of the Atlantic coast by the Europeans, embraced the Seminoles and remnants of tribes of Georgia which had been driven into the peninsula by conquest of their lands above the Savannah River by the whites," and also that "the Seminoles were of the same stock with the Indians who occupied elsewhere the land between the Mississippi River and the seacoast," Allen regards it as probable therefore "that the skulls of the Moore series were of the same stock called by Jones 'Muschogee,' a probability which is strengthened by the statement of Bartram regarding the large stature of the males and the small stature of the females of Muschogee people. The most casual observer of the Moore series will be struck with the disparity in the size of the male and female skulls." This last unaccountable statement, it may be remarked at once, is not sustained by later studies on the collections.

Of the skulls in the Morton collection little is known, according to Allen, "beyond the fact that they were for the most part collected in Florida during or about the time of the Seminole war. Some of them may be from distant tribes which had been driven south, but it is improbable that they belong to other than members of the Muschogee group. That the Moore series differs notably from the skulls marked Seminole is of considerable interest. But the entire number of specimens examined is too small to make any broad deductions."

In 1897 Frank Hamilton Cushing published his "Preliminary Report on the Exploration of Ancient Key-Dweller Remains on the Gulf Coast of Florida,[1] and in it (p. 119) he mentions two series of skulls collected by him on the west coast of the peninsula, one north of Tampa Bay and one at Marco Key among the most northern of the Ten Thousand Islands. In this report also are (105 *et seq.*) two noteworthy discussions on the old dwellers of Florida by the foremost students of such matters at that time,

---

[1] *Proc. Amer. Philos. Soc.*, 1897, xxxv, 120 pp.

Brinton and Putnam. Parts of these discussions will be well worth quoting in these connections, particularly as they are rather hidden in the original.

Brinton, the author of the well-known "History, Tribes and Antiquities of the Floridian Peninsula,"[1] reviews briefly the history and ethnography, as then known, of the territory; expresses the belief that the people of the west coast may have spoken a dialect of the Choctaw (Muskhogean), that their culture pointed in the main in the same direction, and that while there may have been slight contacts with the south there is no evidence of a Carib or Arawak origin of the Floridians.

Professor Putnam referred in particular to a series of skulls collected by Cushing, though in some misapprehension as to their location. His truly noteworthy remarks follow: "Mr. Cushing's collection includes a large number of human skulls which I have had the pleasure of seeing in the museum today. I am much interested to note that these skulls are of the same type as those found in the sand mounds in Florida. The first of this type I ever saw came from the sand mounds around Cedar Keys and were brought to notice by the late Prof. Jeffries Wyman. Mr. Clarence B. Moore has found this type in the sand mounds of eastern Florida. The same general type has been found throughout northern Florida, Georgia, Alabama and through the region extending towards the Cumberland valley in Tennessee; also westward through the Pueblo region and in Central America. It is the general brachycephalic skull; not only brachycephalic but decidedly rounded, with more or less artificial flattening of the frontal and occipital regions. I have regarded this type of skull as belonging to the southern or southwestern peoples of North America. I believe that this type of skull is the type of the people who first settled, so far as we know, in Central America and on the shores of Peru and

---

[1] *O. c.*

northern South America; that in all probability this people extended eastward, coming across the Isthmus through the Central American region and extending along the Gulf of Mexico and over into Florida, and finally, judging from the evidence that Mr. Cushing has presented tonight, being driven on to these keys. In fact, I should consider it probable that the line of migration was directly opposite to this one which has been suggested. That is, I believe it more likely that this was a people who, having had an early home in the Central American region, extended around the Gulf of Mexico, rather than a people who came from South America to the Florida Keys and then spread into Florida and westward."

To which Mr. Cushing answered in part as follows: "If the linguistic evidence relative to connections either toward the north or toward the south, of the ancient key dwellers, is thus far so scant as to be inconclusive, this is to a certain extent also the case with the evidence afforded by the human remains we collected. In justice to Dr. Putnam I must state here that the series of skulls in my collections, examined by him, were not the key-dweller skulls. They were skulls derived from the Anclote region, and like those he mentions as previously collected by Dr. Wyman and Dr. Clarence B. Moore were exhumed from sand mounds. The true key-dweller skulls found by us in the muck beds at Marco and in the bone pit on Sanybel Island, number only 13,[1] but they are pronounced to be, by Dr. Harrison Allen, who is studying them preparatory to full publication,[2] uniformly distinct from those of more northerly and easterly parts of Florida. In the first place, the occipital foramina of these remarkable skulls are abnormally large and remain *open* in even the most mature of them—a characteristic seen in only one

[1] The Sanybel Island is in Charlotte Harbor. It appears that there may have been only two skulls from Key Marco; and today there seem to remain but a few unimportant specimens from Sanybel, preserved in the Wistar Institute, where they were seen by the author.

[2] Harrison Allen's notes on the specimens and illustrations so far could not be located.

cranium of our northern series. In the second place, a curious feature of all these key-dweller skulls is that in no case is the occiput flattened. Finally, they are found to be more nearly of the Antillean type, judged, it is true, by only one or two specimens of the latter examined by Dr. Allen, than of the northern Indian type."

The above records are all that we have on the physical anthropology of the old Floridians or their remains, with the exception of the line of publications that deals with the question of man's antiquity on the peninsula. The latter will be found resumed and critically examined in Bulletins 33 (1907) and 66 (1918) of the Bureau of American Ethnology. These reports, however, while showing that there is no substantial ground for any geological antiquity of man in the peninsula, contribute but little to the anthropology of Florida in general. But their preparation resulted in the several visits of the author to different parts of the State, in the gathering of new evidence as well as skeletal material, and eventually in the present study, the object of which is to bring to date our knowledge of the peopling and peoples of Florida. It will be shown that these problems are probably simpler than may be anticipated, that linguistic evidence has once more proven insufficient, and that observations of untrained men regarding the physical characteristics of a people are wholly unreliable.

NEW OBSERVATIONS

THE present study of skeletal material from Florida included that at the U. S. National Museum, together with all that preserved at the Academy of Natural Sciences and the Wistar Institute in Philadelphia. It comprises the Clarence B. Moore, The Hamilton Cushing,[1] and the author's collections, besides individual specimens from other sources. The small series of skulls previously described by Harrison Allen have been re-examined. The distribution of the utilized skulls is as follows:

CRANIA EXAMINED

	West Coast	St. John's River	East Coast	Southeast and South	Seminoles
Male (121).........	78	16	11	5	11
Female (52).........	33	7	7	3	2
Totals (173).........	111	23	18	8	13

The above represents only normal adult skulls, unaffected by artificial deformation which was practiced more or less in different parts of the peninsula; and not to complicate matters needlessly only the principal measurements and observations will be reported. A large number of other more or less deformed skulls passed through the writer's hands, but the notes on them would be of little value in present connection. In addition there were examined a quantity of other Florida skeletal material than skulls, and all the available crania from neighboring regions.

Deformation.—The majority of Floridian skulls show artificial moulding. There is but one type of this: the fronto-occipital flattening; but in instances the frontal parts have been so little affected that the occipital compression alone is perceptible.

---

[1] A vain search was made for the few skulls believed to have been collected by Cushing at Marco.

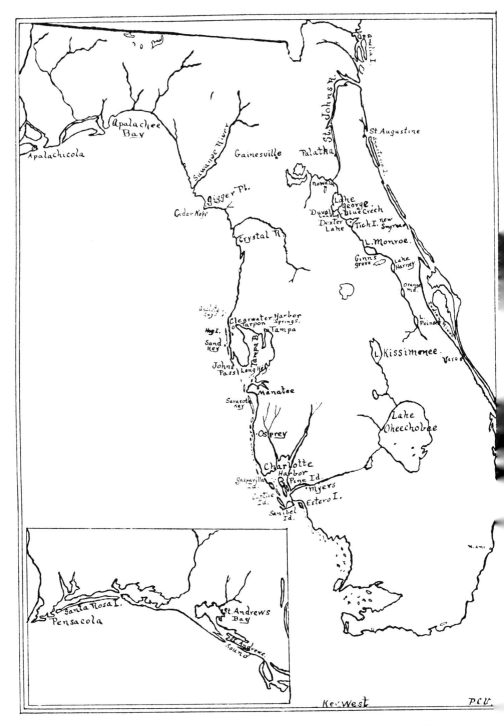

Figure 2. Map of Florida Showing Localities from which Skeletal Material was Examined

The degree and frequency of the deformation differ from locality to locality, both diminishing in general, it appears, from north to south. The "Aymara" type of deformation was unknown and the one or two authors who assumed otherwise were in error. Extreme forms of flattening are absent, and on the whole it is evident that while the practice was wide-spread in Florida, it was rather lax and not seldom neglected or given up.

The same type of head deformation had existed in the territories now covered by Georgia, Alabama, Mississippi, Louisiana and Arkansas. It was also the type of deformation practiced by the stone grave people of Tennessee, and traces of it are occasionally found beyond the boundaries of these states. Its centre of intensity was evidently in the territory now covered by Alabama and Tennessee with adjacent parts of Georgia and Mississippi.

The same type of deformation was general among the Caribs in the Bahamas, Cuba, Haiti, Porto Rico, Jamaica, etc., as well as among the tribes of parts of Central America, in Yucatan, and along portions at least of eastern Mexico; strangely it was also and is to this day practiced in the northwesternmost parts of the United States among the Indians of the Columbia River basin, but nowhere else in North America. In South America it was nearly limited to the upper two-thirds of the western coast.

A deep-rooted complex procedure of this nature implies necessarily close connections of the ancestry of the Florida and related Indians in one or another of these directions, probably even derivation; but the time is not ripe enough as yet for the following of this clue to definite conclusions.

Massiveness.—Many of the Florida skulls and lower jaws as well as the bones of the skeleton impress one as perceptibly stouter and especially heavier than other skeletal remains of Indians. So far as some of the individual skulls and jaws are concerned nothing equally massive is, in fact, known from any part of the continent except under abnormal conditions. The fact, we have seen, has been noted by Wyman as well as Ecker, and is also accentuated by Brooks in his report on some skulls and bones of the Indians of the Bahamas, who evidently belonged to the same type of people.[1]

The stoutness of the skulls was apparent on most of the material that passed through the writer's hands in the present study. The lower parts of the parietal 1 cm. above and along the squamous suture in Florida skulls measured often 6 to 8 mm., which is approximately 2 to 3 mm. more than in the whites and 1.5 mm. more than in other Indians. The occipital crests, the mastoids, the zygomæ in males are often heavier, the facial parts more massive, the lower jaws in general thicker and larger than in most other parts of America. The features in the living must have been correspondingly strong, which, together with a good height of the body, accounts doubtless for the reports by early travellers as to the size and strength of the people, as it accounts for most of the reports of Florida "giants" which are reaching the Press and our Institutions now from amateur explorers.

The explanation of these conditions lies on one hand in a sturdy stock to start with, and on the other in a plentiful supply and the nature of food. The weight of the skulls and bones is, however, not always due to increased thickness, but to mineralization. Outside perhaps of parts of Argentina there is no other large part of the American continent where mineralization of bones is as rapid, as general and also as varied as in Florida. The sands full of shell detritus, the shell mounds, the muck, the brown waters of Florida, all favor infiltration of bones with lime salts as well as other mineral constituents; in other words, a relatively rapid fossilization.

---

[1] Brooks (W. K.). On the Lucayan Indians. *Mem. Nat. Ac. Sc.*, 1889, iv, Pl. 2, 215–222.

In our collection there are human bones from Florida that are almost so much silica, limestone, or iron ore, while one skeleton preserved in the U. S. National Museum is wholly embedded in black, hard manganese sandstone; and there are, as already remarked, few bones from the older mounds or shell heaps that do not show some mineralization. It is these super-added mineral constituents which account in the main for the extraordinary weight of many of the skulls and bones from the peninsula, and it is the additional weight which augments and at times as shown by control measurements, may even be wholly responsible for, the impression of massiveness.

As to the really increased thickness of some of the crania and some of the bones there are, as already implied, reasons to believe that these conditions were not wholly due to muscular strength, though plainly the people and especially the men were sturdy, but that they had considerable to do with the diet of these Indians. This consisted very largely of fish and especially molluscs, both rich in phosphates. The generally more or less mineralized water, too, may have contributed. Whether directly or indirectly, a rich life-long diet with increased intake of bone-forming materials, could hardly fail to affect the skeleton. It is these agencies in the writer's belief that are largely re-sponsible for the massiveness of some of the Florida skeletons. As will be shown later, people of the same physical stock else-where inland, living on a substantially different diet, while also strong and of good stature, had no such thick skulls or bones as some of the Floridians.

Disease.—Next to massiveness the Florida bones from some localities impress one with the commonness of disease. This con-sists essentially of inflammatory processes, periostitis and osteo-periostitis, particularly on the tibia and other long bones. These lesions suggest strongly a syphilitic origin and it would seem that here if anywhere the problem of the presence of pre-Columbian syphilis in America could be settled. But even here the evidence is not conclusive. In the first place there is as yet no decisive proof that the lesions in question are syphilitic, and if the disease was syphilis, as seems likely, then all that can be said positively is that it was prevalent and of a destructive form, as judged by the osseous lesions, *after* the Indian came into contact with the Spaniards, for in many of the mounds with the diseased bones are found articles of white man's introduction. Whether there are any burial mounds in which these bone lesions are completely absent has not yet been determined. All that can be said is that there are localities in Florida from which no diseased bones have been collected. It is strange that no mention of the presence of venereal disease is made in any of the accounts of the peninsula; but the subject of disease has received no attention in these poor records.

Unity of Type.—The third most marked impression made upon the student by the Floridian skeletal material and particularly by the crania, is the similarity of type. The mass of the remains from all parts of the peninsula represented in our collections appear to be clearly those of one well characterized physical strain of people. The more northern parts of the west coast, the Tampa to Charlotte Bay region, the St. John's River, the older parts of the east coast population, all show the same prevailing type of skulls, stature, robustness, form; and measurements only confirm this impression.

Yet here and there is a skull that differs from the rest, shows different outlines, or is in some important respects beyond the ordinary limits of variation; and the proportion of such specimens rises in some spots—especially it seems in the east and towards the south. But there is seldom any sharp line of distinction. In general the odd types connect by imperceptible gradations with the more regular forms, indicating admixture.

And the signs point to a long lasting admixture, though with the odd type as the more recent comer. All of this will be made clearer by the measurements. It will now suffice to say that, as the results of visual observation on Florida skeletal material, we obtain the rather simple impression of one well marked prevalent and older physical type of people; and of a strain smaller in numbers, not far distant in stature and other features, though slightly less robust, coming gradually somewhat later and until fairly recently, admixing here more, here less with the older type, and in some localities even remaining fairly pure. There is no evidence of there having been anything before the older of these two types; and there is no sign of any other intrusion outside of the second contingent.

Our task will be to single out and identify if possible these two peoples.

THE SKULL

The total number of undeformed or nearly undeformed Florida skulls found available for measurement was, as stated, 173, of which 121 males and 52 females; but many of these specimens lacked the facial or basal parts.

The material ranged from specimens enclosed in solidified coquina, and the characteristic dark more or less fossilized skulls from some of the more northern mounds, to the relatively fresh-looking specimens from the shell-heaps of Charlotte Harbor; and the visual impression even more than the measurements spoke for the presence of one prevalent, older, round-headed, with one subsidiary and on the whole fresher, more oblong-headed type. Yet these types occurred nowhere clearly separated, but were well commingled—unless it were in some spots in the south, from which, however, the collections as yet are too scarce to allow of any definite conclusion.

The blackish, brown or grey discoloration of the skulls and bones, with their frequent above-average massiveness accentuated by the increased weight through mineralization, gives the older Florida skeletal remains a characteristic aspect which makes it easy to tell them apart from those of other regions and tends to create an impression of a different variety, a different population than that of the ordinary Indian. Only the fresher material looks like that of other Indians. But detailed observation and especially measurements soon do away with any illusion in these respects.

Another deception that on actual test soon vanished, was that of extraordinary stature, not to speak of giantism. Strong and big men there were, but measurements of the long bones failed to show a single six-footer even, though judging from the averages there may have been occasionally such individuals in the population.

Descriptive Features of the Skull.—The generally defective state of preservation of the Florida material makes anything like a systematic detailed description out of the question; and what there is does not present, outside of the perceptibly greater massiveness in many of the specimens, anything which would not be common also to other Indians of related types.

The vault, looked at from above, is in a large majority of cases a shorter or longer ovoid, approaching in some of the broadest heads to a short elliptical or rounder form (Pl. XII, pl. XIV). The sagittal region is only slightly to moderately raised, not keel shaped. The forehead ranges from rather low to medium, as is usual in Indians. The supra-orbital ridges, as well as the occipital crest, may be heavy in the males, but in no case were they observed to form a complete arch. In females the supra-orbital ridges are generally moderate to small, the occipital crests absent.

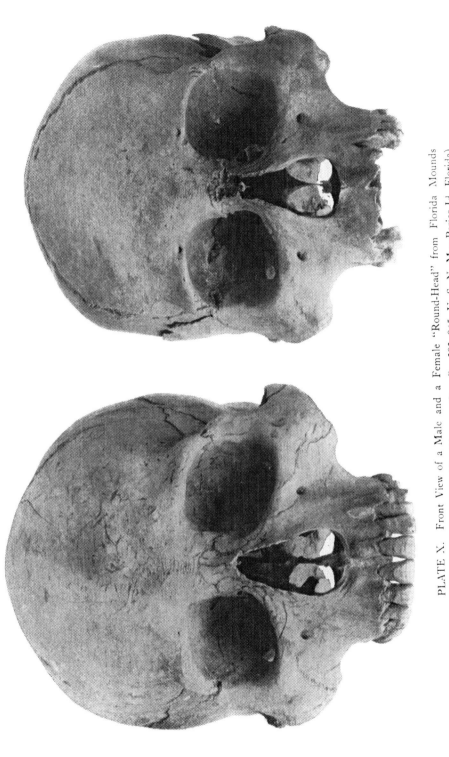

PLATE X. Front View of a Male and a Female "Round-Head" from Florida Mounds
(♂—306, 701, U. S. N. M.—Manatee Co.; ♀—292, 065, U. S. N. M.—Perico Id., Florida)

PLATE XI. Side View of Skulls Shown on PLATES VII. and VIII.

PLATE XII. Top View of Skulls Shown on PLATES VII. and IX.

The facial traits impress one by the strength of the zygomæ, malars and dental arch; the lower jaw by its general strength and size. In a few instances the lower jaw is truly enormous (Pl. XVII, pl. XVIII).

The orbits are variable, ranging from mesoseme to megaseme. The nose, moderately raised and moderately broad, is frequently rather long. The nasal spine is generally low; the lower borders of the nasal aperture range from fairly well marked to dull. Alveolar prognathism is somewhat more marked than in whites, as usual in Indians. Teeth are meso- to macrodont, typically Indian.

The mastoids are about as the average in Indians, occasionally somewhat heavier. The features of the base of the skull in general are heavier than usual, but otherwise typically Indian.

The more rounded skulls on the one hand and the more oblong ones on the other, show each a considerable uniformity of type; furthermore, except in the relative length and breadth of the vault and in the lesser general massiveness of the more oblong skulls, there are no great differences and no real separation between the two varieties, the space being filled by intermediary forms. It is plain that, to start with, the two elements entering into the Florida population did not differ much in their facial features; and that there has been a prolonged commingling of the stronger older, and the newer strains, resulting in numerous more or less intermediary forms; though the mixture has not been sufficient to obliterate fully or even greatly the original two types.

Measurements.—The principal measurements on the undeformed Florida crania show remarkable features with which we have thus far been but little acquainted on this continent. In size of the vault the skulls compare favorably with those of other Indian tribes. They are both externally and internally slightly larger than those of some other Indians, but this is essentially a matter of bulk and stature; where those were similar the size of the head is similar. There were some macrocephals, also now and then a microcephal among the Floridians, but the mass of the crania show typical Indian dimensions. The 96 Eastern States crania (north of the Carolinas) reported upon by the writer in 1916,[1] gave the average cranial module or mean diameter $\frac{(L + B + H)}{(3)}$ of 15.54 cm., while 76 male Florida skulls give 15.52 cm.; the average module of 100 female eastern crania was 14.78, that of 34 Florida skulls of the same sex 14.93 cm; and the capacity agreement is similar. Nineteen male skulls from Arkansas and Louisiana gave the module of 15.49 cm. with a capacity of 1456 c.c.—11 Florida skulls of the same sex[2] in which the capacity could be determined gave respectively 15.63 cm. and 1478 c.c. for the same measurements; or taking the largest series of our eastern skulls, the 30 female crania from New Jersey,[3] we find the average module of 14.70 cm. with the mean capacity of 1306 c.c., while 7 Florida female skulls in which the capacity could well be measured gave a module of 14.85 cm. and capacity of 1318 c.c. Whatever excess in general there appears in favor of Florida may be attributed in all probability either to insufficiency of the numbers of specimens available for comparison, or to an excess of size and weight of the Floridians.

The outstanding feature of the Florida crania appears not in size but in the measurements relating to their form. The skulls are both absolutely and relatively *very high*. Curiously, moreover, this applies to both of the types of skull occurring in the peninsula, the rounded as well as the more oblong.

[1] Physical Anthropology of the Lenape or Delawares and of the Eastern Indians in General. Bull. 62, Bur. Am. Ethnol., 8°, Washington, 1916, 118.

[2] Leaving out two exceptional macrocephalic specimens.

[3] Bull. 62, B. A. E., 119.

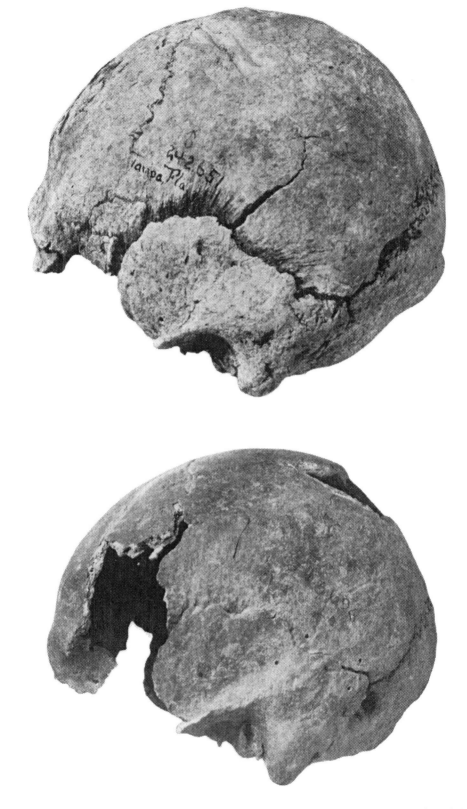

PLATE XIII. Side View of a Male (upper) and a Female (lower) Florida Skull of the Rounded
Type

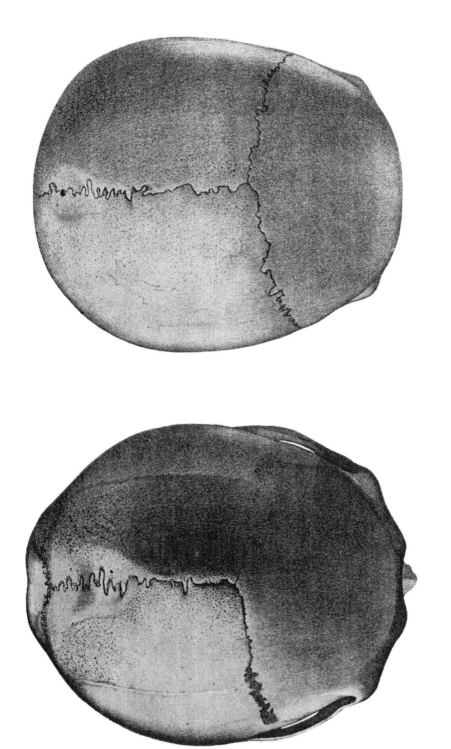

PLATE XIV. Male and a Female "Round-Head" from the St. Johns River Mounds (C. B. Moore, collector), Florida. (After Harrison Allen)

PLATE XV. Florida Crania: The Rounded and the Oblong Types

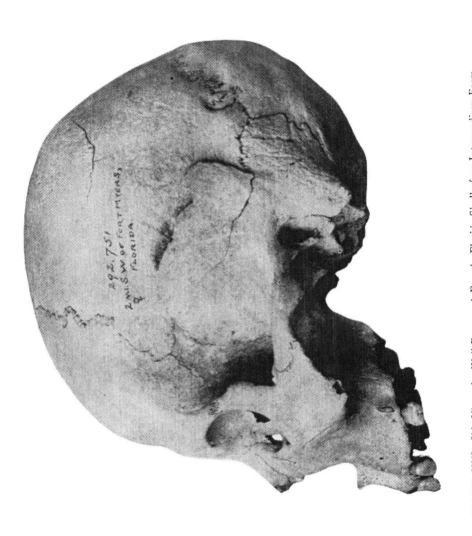

PLATE XVI. Side View of a Well-Preserved Female Florida Skull of an Intermediary Form

This characteristic is so marked and universal in the peninsula as to constitute a prominent mark which should prove of much value in tracing the origin and relations of the population.

The feature is best expressed by the *Mean Height Index* $\frac{(H)}{(Mean\ of\ L + B)}$. Advocated independently by the writer first in 1916,[1] this Index is proving of much value in differentiation of type and will probably become a permanent feature in Craniometry.

The conditions, taking all the Florida crania together, are shown in the following tables: p, 94 et seq.

An effort to separate the two types of skulls, the older more rounded and the evidently more recent and more oblong, by measurements, meets with only a partial success due to the proximity of the two forms in many respects. Visual observations are here more efficient. They make it plain that the rounded type extended its normal range of variation from a high brachy- into mesocephaly, while on the other hand the more oblong type, apparently sub-dolicho- to mesocephalic in its pure state, reached occasionally into sub-brachycephaly. But the mixed forms, as has already been stated, bridge over the separation.

The tables following p. 98 show some of the differences as well as the overlapping of the two types. The oblong heads appear to be both longer as well as narrower than those of the more rounded variety, and they are both absolutely and relatively even higher than the former, but in size of the facial and nasal measurements the two types show much parallelism.

A good fortune was to find in the collections eleven male skulls of the Seminoles together, the measurements of which

---

[1] Bull. 62, B. A. E., 116.

UNDEFORMED FLORIDA CRANIA: MEASUREMENTS RELATING TO THE FORM AND SIZE OF THE VAULT

	Length (a)	Breadth (b)	Height (basion-bregma) (c)	Cephalic Index $\frac{(b \times 100)}{a}$	Height-Length Index $\frac{(c \times 100)}{a}$	Height-Breadth Index $\frac{(c \times 100)}{b}$	Mean Height Index $\frac{(c \times 100)}{(\text{mean of a \& b})}$	Cranial Module $\frac{(L + B + H)}{3}$	Capacity* (Hrdlička's method)
				MALES					
Average	(110) 17.97	(110) 14.53	(76) 14.17	(110) 80.8	(76) 79.-	(76) 98.3	(76) 87.6	(76) 15.52	(13) 1513
Minimum	16.5	13.2	13.1	73.7	70.7	87.8	80.1	14.60	1435
Maximum	19.3	16.-	15.5	88.9	85.1	108.8	94.6	16.47	1745
				FEMALES					
Average	(50) 17.1	(50) 13.9	(34) 13.55	(50) 81.5	(34) 78.6	(34) 94.8	(34) 87.2	(34) 14.93	(7) 1318
Minimum	15.8	12.9	12.6	75.6	72.9	88.9	81.4	13.80	1215
Maximum	18.1	14.8	14.8	83.-	86.8	105.3	93.6	15.63	1360

* That of the skulls measured in Philadelphia could not be taken.

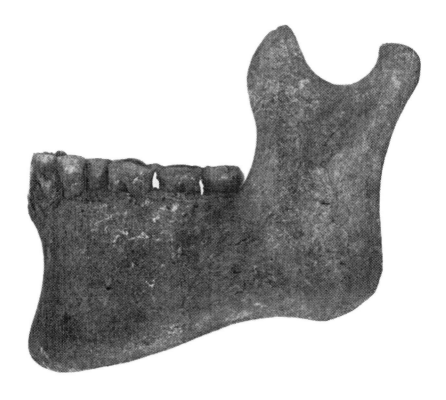

PLATE XVII. Extraordinary Lower Jaw from the Florida Mounds—Full Size

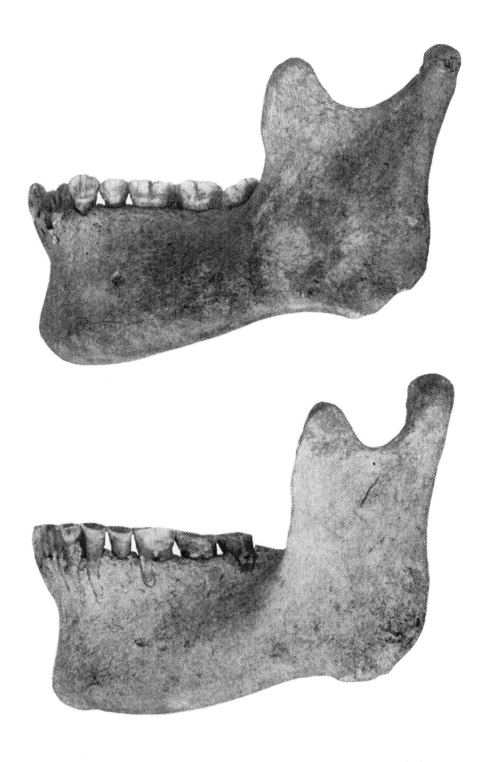

PLATE XVIII. Extraordinary Lower Jaws from the Florida Mounds—Full Size

FLORIDA BRACHYCEPHALIC CONTRASTED WITH FLORIDA MESOCEPHALIC AND NARROWER CRANIA

	Vault:								Face:					Nose:		
	L.	B.	H.	C.I.	H.L.I.	H.B.I.	Mean Height Index	Cran. Mod.	Ment. Nas.	Alv. Pt. Nas.	D. bizyg. max.	F.I. tot.	F.I. upper	L.	B.	N.I.
MALES																
C.I. 80 & above	(69) 17.87	(69) 14.71	(46) 14.13	(69) 82.4	(46) 79.3	(46) 96.6	(46) 87.1	(46) 15.52	(10) 12.64	(33) 7.49	(36) 14.28	(10) 88.-	(31) 52.5	(41) 5.29	(39) 2.48	(39) 47.-
C.I. below 80	(40) 18.24	(40) 14.20	(29) 14.23	(40) 77.9	(29) 78.5	(29) 100.8	(29) 88.1	(29) 15.52	(7) 12.30	(20) 7.40	(17) 13.96	(7) 87.9	(14) 52.-	(22) 5.22	(22) 2.48	(22) 47.6
Seminoles	(11) 17.91	(11) 13.80	(11) 13.89	(11) 77.-	(11) 77.6	(11) 100.7	(11) 87.6	(11) 15.20	—	(11) 7.1	(11) 13.5	—	(11) 52.5	(10) 5.18	(10) 2.62	(10) 50.6
FEMALES																
C.I. 80 & above	(31) 16.90	(31) 14.10	(21) 13.54	(31) 83.5	(21) 80.4	(21) 96.5	(21) 87.7	(21) 14.81	(3) 11.93	(9) 6.9	(7) 13.3	(3) 89.1	(6) 52.7	(12) 4.98	(9) 2.36	(9) 46.9
C.I. below 80	(18) 17.40	(18) 13.60	(12) 13.50	(18) 78.4	(12) 78.1	(12) 99.8	(12) 87.6	(12) 14.79	(2) 10.9	(6) 7.-	(3) 13.6	—	(3) 50.7	(6) 5.02	(5) 2.34	(5) 46.4

Seminoles (not enough specimens for comparison).*

* For measurements on 2 female adults and 2 female adolescents see detailed measurements.

are here given for comparison. The data will be discussed later; but it will be seen at a glance that the Seminole crania show a considerable resemblance to the oblong Florida skulls of older extraction. This relation helps materially to sustain the distinctness of the oblong cranial type of the mounds and shell heaps from the more rounded form, and indicates strongly where lie the relations and possibly derivation of the former.

In seriation (table p. 97) and in the more detailed graphic outline of the distribution of the cephalic index in Florida (Fig. 3) there is noticeable a tendency towards a double grouping, one in mesocephaly and one in brachycephaly, which also supports the deduction of the presence in mixture of two separate forms of skull.

The mean height index, which may well be studied in the males, shows a considerable range of distribution, with marked aggregation between 86 and 88 or more broadly between 85 and 89 (p. 100). The seriation gives nowhere more than one mode, indicating that in this respect the more rounded and the more oblong types of skulls are much alike (Fig. 4). Taken separately the more oblong skulls are seen to be even slightly higher, and that both relatively and absolutely, than those of the rounded type, which is a fact of some importance (table p. 95).

After having reached satisfying evidence of the existence in the mounds and shell heaps of Florida of two distinct though admixed cranial forms representing two component strains of population, the next point of importance was to determine if possible the original distribution of the rounded and the oblong skulls over the peninsula.

During the examination it soon became obvious that the oblong forms of skull were relatively more frequent in certain eastern and in the southern parts of the peninsula, than else-

FLORIDA MOUND AND SHELL-HEAP SKULLS (ALL)—DISTRIBUTION OF CRANIAL INDEX

	73.7 -74	74.1 -75	75.1 -76	76.1 -77	77.1 -78	78.1 -79	79.1 -80	80.1 -81	81.1 -82	82.1 -83	83.1 -84	84.1 -85	85.1 -86	86.1 -87	87.1 -88	88.1 -89	89.1 -90
MALES																	
WEST COAST (78)	1	—	1	5	5	4	14	11	17	4	8	4	1	—	2	1	—
ST. JOHNS R. (16)	—	—	—	1	1	—	—	2	5	3	1	1	—	2	—	—	—
EAST COAST & SO. FLA. (16)	—	1	—	2	5	—	3	1	1	3	—	—	—	—	—	—	—
TOTAL (110)	1	1	1	8	11	4	17	14	23	10	9	5	1	2	2	1	—
PERCENT	.9	.9	.9	7.2	10.-	3.6	15.4	12.7	20.9	9.09	8.1	4.5	.9	1.8	1.8	.9	—
FEMALES																	
WEST COAST & ST. JOHNS R. (40)	—	—	1	1	4	4	6	1	6	4	2	4	3	1	2	—	1
EAST COAST & SO. FLA. (10)	—	—	—	1	—	2	—	1	2	3	1	—	—	—	—	—	—
TOTAL (50)	—	—	1	2	4	6	6	2	8	7	3	4	3	1	2	—	1
PERCENT	—	—	2.0	4.0	8.0	12.0	12.0	4.0	16.0	14.0	6.0	8.0	6.0	2.0	4.0	—	2.0
SEMINOLES																	
SEMINOLES MALES (11)	1	2	1	2	2	1	1	1	—	—	—	—	—	—	—	—	—

FLORIDA CRANIA: MEAN HEIGHT INDEX

$$\left(\frac{H}{\text{Mean of } L + B}\right)$$

More Compact Grouping (in Males)

	80.1-82.5	82.6-85	85.1-87.5	87.6-90	90.1-92.5	92.6-95
MALES (76)	3	8	31	20	11	3
PERCENT	*3.9*	*10.5*	*40.8*	*26.3*	*14.5*	*3.9*
FEMALES (34)	4	3	7	11	8	1
PERCENT	*11.8*	*8.8*	*20.6*	*32.3*	*23.5*	*2.9*

Detailed Grouping (in Males)

	80.1 -81	81.1 -82	82.1 -83	83.1 -84	84.1 -85	85.1 -86	86.1 -87	87.1 -88	88.1 -89	89.1 -90	90.1 -91	91.1 -92	92.1 -93	93.1 -94	94.1 -94.6
WEST COAST & ST. JOHNS R. (63)	—	2	1	2	5	5	12	14	4	8	3	3	3	—	1
EAST COAST & S. FLORIDA (13)	1	—	—	—	—	3	1	3	4	1	1	1	—	2	—
TOTAL (76)	1	2	1	2	5	8	13	17	4	9	4	4	3	2	1
PERCENT	*1.3*	*2.6*	*1.3*	*2.6*	*6.6*	*10.5*	*17.1*	*22.4*	*5.3*	*11.8*	*5.3*	*5.3*	*3.9*	*2.6*	*1.3*
SEMINOLES (11)	—	1	—	—	—	2	2	2	2	—	—	—	2	—	—

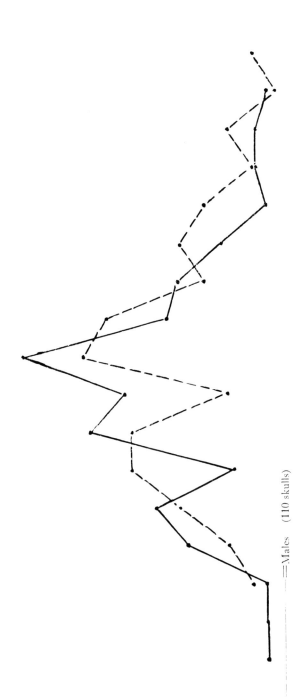

Cranial Index of Florida Crania (all)
from Mounds and Shell Heaps

——— Males (110 skulls)
·········· Females (50 ")

.

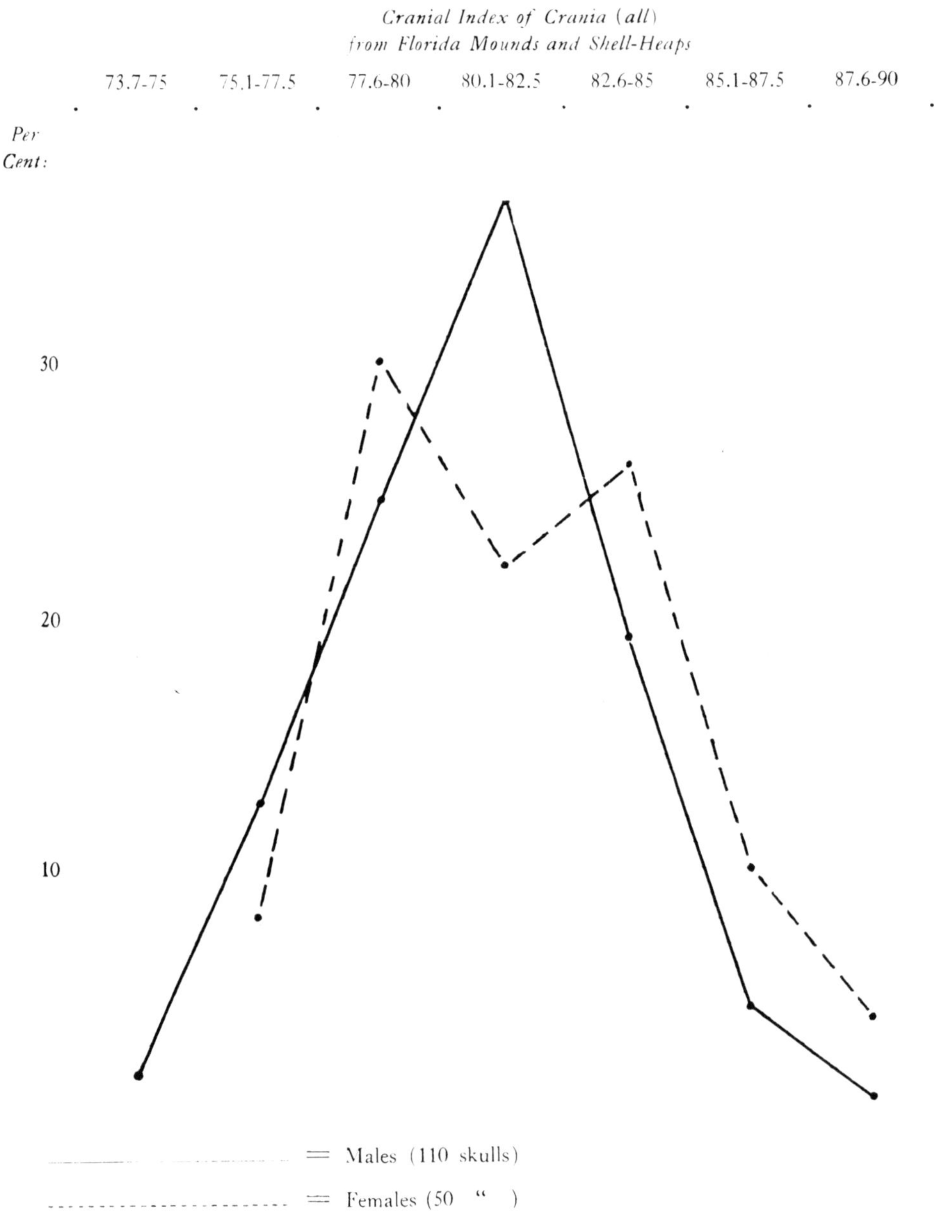

Cranial Index of Crania (all)
from Florida Mounds and Shell-Heaps

| 73.7-75 | 75.1-77.5 | 77.6-80 | 80.1-82.5 | 82.6-85 | 85.1-87.5 | 87.6-90 |

Per
Cent:

30

20

10

——————— = Males (110 skulls)

- - - - - - - - - = Females (50 ")

Fig. 3b

where; but unfortunately these parts are much less well represented in our collections than the regions further west and north,
which makes it hard to draw valid conclusions, and to say
whether the oblong type was anywhere present exclusively.

In order to obtain as much light on the subject as possible,
the available cranial material was divided into several groups,
corresponding to the traditionally and otherwise most important parts of the territory. These regions are respectively the
West Coast or the Caloosa country; the St. John's River and the
remaining region of the Timucua tribes; the East Coast; and the
Southeast with the South. The data may be consulted in the following tables which give us it is seen several valuable indications.

The West Coast and the St. John's River regions are, whatever linguistic or other differences there may have been between
them, from the standpoint of physical anthropology practically
identical. Both show the presence and influence of the oblong
heads, but the type is substantially that of the old brachycephals.
The East Coast also is prevalently the same, but along this coast
and from Lake Okechobee southward there becomes apparent a
greater infusion of the more oblong high type of skulls, and there
are spots where this type may even have been present alone.

Facial Proportions.—The facial measurements of the Florida
skulls show, too, some points of special interest, though in general
representing well in every particular the Indian type.

The measurements show the face to be both high and rather
broad; the relative proportions, as expressed by the indices, are,
however, quite usual. The breadth of the face is to that of the
skull as approximately 97.5 to 100 in the males and as 96 to 100
in the females—for Indians not very unusual proportions.

In conformity with the high face we have also a rather high
nose, with medium breadth, giving in both sexes a fairly low
nasal index. Under ordinary conditions a low or even a moderate

UNDEFORMED FLORIDA CRANIA—MALES

	Vault:								Face:					Nose:		
	L.	B.	H.	C.I.	H.L.I.	H.B.I.	Mean H.I.	Cran. Mod.	Ment. Nas.	Alv. Pt. Nas.	D. bizyg. max.	F.I. tot.	F.I. upper	L.	B.	N.I.
	cm.	cm.	cm.					cm.	cm.	cm.	cm.			cm.	cm.	
MEANS, WEST COAST	(78) 17.99	(78) 14.53	(55) 14.14	(55) 80.8	(55) 79.-	(55) 98.2	(55) 87.6	(55) 15.48	(12) 12.56	(44) 7.47	(40) 14.1	(10) 88.9	(37) 52.6	(47) 5.29	(47) 2.5	(47) 47.3
ST. JOHNS RIVER	(16) 17.96	(16) 14.75	(8) 14.2	(16) 81.5	(8) 78.6	(8) 96.4	(8) 86.6	(8) 15.67	—	(4) 7.4	(5) 14.9	—	(4) 49.5	(6) 5.2	(4) 2.35	(4) 45.9
EAST COAST	(11) 18.09	(11) 14.44	(10) 14.22	(11) 79.8	(10) 78.6	(10) 98.4	(10) 87.4	(10) 15.59	(3) 12.-	(4) 7.45	(5) 14.-	(2) 85.9	(2) 55.1	(8) 5.3	(8) 2.55	(8) 48.2
SOUTH FLORIDA	(5) 18.08	(5) 13.96	(3) 14.56	(5) 77.2	(3) 80.5	(3) 104.3	(3) 90.9	(3) 15.54	(4) 12.3	(2) 7.55	(4) 13.9	(4) 88.8	(2) 54.4	(4) 5.1	(4) 2.46	(4) 48.-

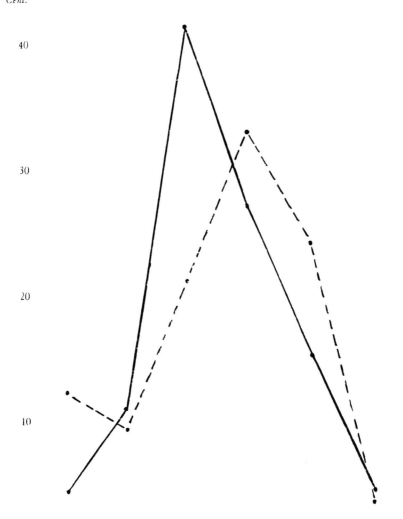

Mean Height Index of Skulls (all)
from Florida Mounds and Shell Heaps

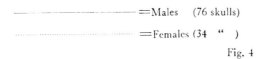
=Males   (76 skulls)
=Females (34 "   )

Fig. 4

UNDEFORMED FLORIDA CRANIA—FEMALES

	Vault:								Face:					Nose:		
	L.	B.	H.	C.I.	H.L.I.	H.B.I.	Mean H.I.	Cran. Mod.	Ment. Nas.	Alv. Pt. Nas.	D. bizyg. max.	F.I. tot.	F.I. upper	L.	B.	N.I.
	cm.	cm.	cm.					cm.	cm.	cm.	cm.			cm.	cm.	
MEANS, WEST COAST	(33) 17.23	(33) 14.-	(21) 13.56	(33) 81.2	(21) 77.4	(21) 97.2	(21) 86.2	(21) 15.02	(6) 11.4	(13) 7.-	(9) 13.4	(5) 87.-	(9) 52.4	(15) 5.05	(15) 2.4	(15) 47.5
ST. JOHNS RIVER	(7) 16.94	(7) 14.11	(5) 13.56	(7) 83.3	(5) 80.-	(5) 96.7	(5) 87.5	(5) 14.85								
EAST COAST	(7) 16.97	(7) 13.75	(5) 13.62	(7) 81.1	(5) 80.1	(5) 99.6	(5) 88.8	(5) 14.78		(2) 7.15	(2) 13.05		(2) 54.8	(3) 5.1		
SOUTH FLORIDA	(2) 16.75	(2) 13.3	(2) 13.55	(3) 80.5	(3) 81.9	(3) 101.8	(3) 90.8	(2) 14.53								

nasal index in tribes living so far south would strongly suggest a northern rather than a southern derivation, and that within not very far distant times, for of all features of the skull the proportions and particularly the width of the nasal aperture bear probably on the whole the closest relation to environmental conditions, more particularly heat and humidity. But the moderate nasal index of the Floridians is due essentially to the increased height of the face which affects all its parts including the nose. The Floridian nose must therefore be described as high and not narrow.

The alveolar and facial angles, and the dimensions of the palate as well as those of the teeth, could be studied on account of the very frequent damage or absence of the facial parts on only a few specimens, where they showed ordinary Indian conditions; and the same applies to the orbits.

An abstract of the main facial measurements together with their distribution is given in the following tables.

The lower jaws from the Florida mounds deserve more than a passing notice; not so much from the racial standpoint, perhaps, but on account of the individual variation and their development, this last reaching in some instances truly remarkable proportions.

Except in the physically weakest tribes north of Mexico, the Indian lower jaw averages distinctly larger and heavier in both sexes than that in the working classes of any American whites. The conditions are shown best in the second of the following three tables. Of the six principal dimensions of the lower jaw, in only one, the height of the ascending ramus—a dimension depending more on the length of the face than on the strength of the mandible—does the lower jaw of the whites come near the general Indian average; in all the rest of the measurements the Indian jaw is the larger and heavier. And the Florida lower jaws,

FLORIDA SKULLS: MEASUREMENTS RELATING TO THE FACE

	Face: Height Menton-Nasion (a)	Height Alveolar Pt.-Nasion (b)	Diameter Bizygomatic maximum (c)	Facial Index Total $\frac{a \times 100}{c}$	Facial Index Upper $\frac{b \times 100}{c}$	Nose: Length	Breadth	Nasal Index
MALES								
Average	(19) 12.4	(54) 7.47	(54) 14.14	(16) 83.3	(45) 52.5	(65) 5.27	(63) 2.49	(63) 47.4
Minimum	11.4	6.6	12.7	79.6	47.3	4.6	2.1	38.6
Maximum	13.3	8.1	15.4	94.7	61.1	5.9	3.-	56.6
FEMALES								
Average	(6) 11.4	(15) 7.-	(12) 13.34	(5) 87.-	(9) 52.4	(14) 5.05	(15) 2.4	(15) 47.5
Minimum	10.8	6.3	12.8	80.9	48.9	4.6	2.-	40.8
Maximum	12.3	7.6	13.9	90.9	56.8	5.4	2.6	52.-

SERIATION

THE UPPER FACIAL INDEX $\left(\dfrac{Alveolar\ Pt.\text{-}Nasion \times 100}{Diam.\ bizygom.\ max.}\right)$

	45.1–47.5	47.6–50	50.1–52.5	52.6–55	55.1–57.5	57.6–60	60.1–62.5
MALES (45)	2	10	10	11	10	1	1
Percent:	4.4	22.2	22.2	24.6	22.2	2.2	2.2
FEMALES (11)	—	3	3	2	3	—	—
Percent:	—	27.3	27.3	18.2	27.3	—	—

THE NASAL INDEX

	Below 40	40.1–42.5	42.6–45	45.1–47.5	47.6–50	50.1–52.5	52.6–55	55.1–57.5
MALES (63)	1	3	11	21	15	5	3	4
Percent	1.6	4.8	17.5	33.4	23.8	7.9	4.8	6.3
FEMALES (17)	—	3	2	2	7	3	—	—
Percent:	—	17.6	11.7	11.7	41.2	17.6	—	—

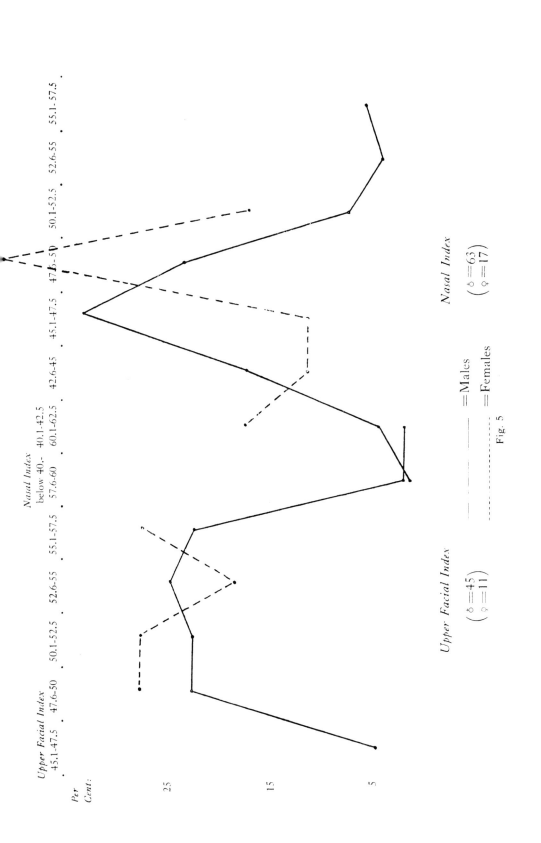

Fig. 5

together with the related Louisiana lot and with those of our most robust Plains tribe, the Sioux, stand in all these respects at the head of the Indians, and that, there are reasons to believe, not merely at the head of those available for comparison but probably of North American Indians in general.

As to some of the individual jaws from Florida, there are five in the U. S. National Museum that are truly huge. Their measurements are given separately in the third of the tables that follow, but the visual impression they produce is even greater. There is nothing that would equal these specimens as a whole in the National Museum collections, except a fresh jaw of a Mongolian collected by the writer in 1912 at Urga.[1] It is small wonder that amateur collectors in Florida finding now and then such a jaw, attribute it to "giants." As a matter of fact none of these specimens proceed, so far as can be determined, from men of any extraordinary stature, but doubtless their owners were powerful individuals.

Large, powerful individual jaws are met with also in the mound remains from Arkansas and Louisiana and over the rest of the region occupied once by the strong southern brachy-cephals. They mean powerful muscles of mastication, as well as abundant nourishment of the bone-forming nature, rather than any distinct physical type. Exceptionally strong specimens, though not perhaps equalling the Florida maximum, may occasionally be met with in other robust Indian tribes, regardless of their derivation.

In one of the Florida jaws, No. 242,632 N. M., otherwise not massive or above the Florida average,[2] the symphyseal height is no less than 4.95 cm.—possibly a unique proportion. The total

---

[1] No. 278,790; D. ant. post. 8.4; d. bigon. 12.; height at symph. 4.2; h. of l. asc. ramus 7.7; breath min. of asc. ram. 4.05; thickn. oppos. mid. of 2 l. molar 2. cm.

[2] D. a-p. 7.8; d. big. 11.6; h. of l. asc. r. 7.3; br. min. of asc. r. 3.4; thickn. at 2 l. mol. 1.4 cm.

Florida: Lower Jaw

	Diameter, Antero-posterior of whole jaw*	Diameter bigonial	Height at symphisis	Height of left ascending ramus	Breadth minimum of ascending ramus mean cf r. & l.	Thickness of jaw at middle of 2nd l. molar
			MALE			
Average	(24) 8.45	(22) 10.75	(29) 3.69	(18) 6.72	(29) 3.73	(29) 1.66
Minimum	7.3	9.6	3.-	5.6	3.2	1.25
Maximum	9.6	12.1	4.95	7.6	4.5	2.-
			FEMALE			
Average	(19) 7.72	(17) 9.7	(21) 3.58	(18) 6.02	(21) 3.44	1.50
Minimum	6.7	8.2	3.-	5.3	2.7	1.1
Maximum	8.4	10.7	3.9	6.8	4.-	1.8

*most posterior points on the condyles and on ... the horizontal rami ... of the chin to middle of base line of oblique plane applied from behind to the ...

FLORIDA LOWER JAWS COMPARED WITH THOSE OF OTHER INDIANS AND WHITES

Locality & Number of Specimens	Diameter antero-posterior of Whole Jaw	Diameter Bigonial	Height at Symphysis	Height of Left Ascending Ramus	Breadth Minimum of Ascending Ramus Mean of r. & l.	Thickness of Jaw at r. angles to Middle of 2nd left Molar
MALE						
Florida (29)	*8.45*	*10.75*	*3.69*	*6.72*	*3.78*	*1.66*
Munsee (9)	8.–	10.5	3.7	6.41	3.5	1.5
Kentucky (44)	7.45	10.5	3.49	6.48	3.44	1.47
Arkansas (62)	7.88	10.5	3.65	6.52	3.47	1.52
Louisiana (21)	8.44	10.7	3.75	7.–	3.72	1.63
Sioux (36)	8.49	10.6	3.6	6.72	3.8	1.6
U. S. Whites (misc.) (50)	**7.57**	**10.1**	**3.29**	**6.53**	**3.15**	**1.45**
FEMALE						
Florida (28)	*7.72*	*9.7*	*3.38*	*6.02*	*3.44*	*1.5*
Munsee (7)	7.2	9.6	3.4	5.56	3.2	1.5
Kentucky (30)	7.12	9.45	3.18	5.64	3.2	1.42
Arkansas (61)	7.5	9.6	3.43	5.85	3.24	1.47
Louisiana (19)	7.38	9.9	3.4	5.73	3.28	1.53
Sioux (27)	7.88	9.9	3.22	6.07	3.69	1.5
U. S. Whites (misc.) (25)	**7.02**	**9.1**	**2.85**	**5.87**	**2.85**	**1.28**

INDIVIDUAL FLORIDA LOWER JAWS*

MALE

No. U.S.N.M.	Locality	Diameter, Antero-posterior, of whole jaw	Diameter, bigonial	Height at Symphysis	Height of left ascending ramus	Breadth minimum of ascending ramus mean of r. & l.	Thickness of jaw at middle of 2nd left molar
292,754	Charlotte Bay	8.3	11.7	3.8	7.4	3.7	1.95
35,946	Tampa Bay	8.7	10.7	3.9	6.7	4.3	1.9
242,633	Pensacola Bay	9.4	12.1	4.-	7.-	4.4	1.85
227,307	Clearwater	—	—	—	7.6	4.-	1.7
315,495	Indian Hill	9.6	10.-	3.7	—	4.1	1.7
Mean of Florida Males		8.45	10.75	3.69	6.72	3.78	1.66

* Those markedly exceptional specimens were not included into the series recorded in the preceding table.

height of the face in this case is 15.1 cm., that from the alveolar point to nasion 8.9 cm.—with the maximum bizygomatic breadth of 13.6 cm. The specimen is not acromegalic.

Comparative.—Summarizing briefly the results of the cranial measurements, we see that the Florida skulls are essentially brachycephalic and mesocephalic, the dolichocephalic element being almost wholly absent; that in general they are both absolutely and relatively high; that notwithstanding their above-average massiveness they are of good capacity; that the face is both high as well as fairly broad; and that the nose is high with medium breadth, giving, for Indians, a fairly low nasal index.

We have seen further that it was possible to distinguish in the remains two separate, though mixed and in many respects connecting types—the prevalent and probably on the whole older more round-headed, and the less frequent and evidently somewhat more recent to recent oblong-headed variety. The next problems that confront us are the determinations of the identity, relations and spread of these types.

Had we ample skeletal material from all the southern States as well as from the Antilles and eastern Mexico, the above tasks would be very simple. As it is we are still far from this goal, and we are even poorer in measurements on the living remnants of the various tribes that survive in these regions. In trying to identify the Floridians, therefore, the anthropologist is confronted with serious difficulties. From many localities there are mere samplings of skeletal remains and from the larger part of the Antilles and practically the whole of eastern Mexico there is nothing whatever. And yet there are, thanks mainly to the assiduous labors of Mr. Clarence B. Moore and further north of Professor F. W. Putnam, precious collections which, with the relatively abundant material from the eastern and central States, as well as further westward, enable us to approach at least some definite conclusions.

As to further South the material at our disposal includes some imperfect specimens from Cuba, even less from Santo Domingo, a few skulls from Jamaica and a small series of modern crania from Yucatan. In all these localities we meet with the same type of artificial cranial deformation as in Florida. All of the available non-deformed skulls are brachycephalic and very similar in many respects; but they are all less thick and robust and perceptibly smaller—proceeding from smaller people—than the Floridian skulls, and what differentiates them definitely from these is that they are all both absolutely and relatively to the other measurements, decidedly lower. Outside of brachycephaly and of the similarity of artificial deformation, there is therefore thus far no strong lead that would point to the derivation of either one of the Florida types of skulls from the southward.

To the North and Northwest of the peninsula the indications are very different. A few imperfect specimens from South Carolina appear to show the same brachycephalic type as that of Florida. A little larger collection from Georgia shows the same type to the point of identity, including the artificial deformation; and the same is true of some skulls from Alabama and parts of Mississippi. Due to Mr. Clarence B. Moore's assiduous efforts we are much more fortunate with collections from Arkansas and Louisiana—and a comparison of the prevailing, brachycephalic, high-skulled type of those regions shows an exceedingly close relation of the same with that of the Floridians. From Texas, regrettably, we have hardly anything as yet in the way of older skulls or skeletons. But there is collectively a riches of material from Tennessee, and the prevalent brachycephalic part of this material—in the undeformed skulls —shows conclusively that it also belongs to the same type as the main strain of Florida.

PERI-FLORIDIAN CRANIA, UNDEFORMED—AVERAGES

MALES

Locality Tribe	Number of Specimen	Vault: L.	B.	H.	C.I.	H-L-I	H-B-I	Mean H-I	Cranial Module	Face: Menton Nasion	Alv. Pt.-Nas.	D. bizyg. max.	F.I. total	F.I. upper	Nasal Aperture: H.	B.	N.I.
S. Carolina	(1)	17.4	15.9	14.5	91.4	83.3	91.2	87.1	15.93	—	—	—	—	—	—	—	—
Georgia	(3)	17.67	14.07	14.57	79.8*	82.6	103.6	91.9	15.46	—	7.6	14.2	—	53.6	5.4	2.6	47.8
Alabama	(3)	17.5	14.7	14.13	84.2	80.9	96.1	87.9	15.43	—	7.4	13.75	—	53.8	5.03	2.5	49.8
Tennessee	(21)**	16.7	14.6	14.20	87.2	85.-	97.6	90.9	15.17	12.1	7.4	13.9	86.-	53.7	5.2	2.6	50.-
Mississippi	(1)	18.3	15.3	14.8	83.6	80.9	96.7	88.1	16.13	—	—	—	—	—	—	—	—
Arkansas	(12)**	17.43	14.63	14.16	84.-	81.7	96.6	88.5	15.39	11.96	7.24	13.9	85.8	52.-	5.13	2.58	50.2
Louisiana	(10)**	17.8	14.63	14.77	82.9	83.-	100.9	91.4	15.55	12.35	7.55	14.2	86.-	53.-	5.16	2.62	50.9
Florida	(69)**	17.9	14.7	14.13	82.4	79.3	96.6	87.1	15.52	12.64	7.49	14.28	88.-	52.5	5.29	2.48	47.-

* Includes C.I.'s of 77.-, 79.8 and 82.6, but skulls are plainly of one type.

** C. I. 80 and above.

PERI-FLORIDIAN CRANIA, UNDEFORMED—AVERAGES

FEMALES

Locality Tribe	Number of Specimens	Vault:							Cranial Module	Face:					Nasal Aperture:		
		L.	B.	H.	C. I.	H-L-I	H-B-I	Mean H-I		Menton Nasion	Alv. Pt. -Nas.	D. bizyg. Max.	F. I. total	F. I. upper	H.	B.	N. I.
Georgia	(3)	16.4	13.6	13.87	82.9	84.6	101.-	92.5	14.62	—	7.03	13.27	—	53.-	5.-	2.33	46.7
Alabama	(3)	16.9	14.2	13.7	84.2	81.-	96.2	88.-	14.91	11.6	7.1	13.4	85.8	53.1	5.03	2.47	49.-
Alabama Choctaw	(2)	16.4	13.7	13.5	83.5	82.3	98.5	89.7	14.53	(11.4)	6.9	12.15	—	56.7	(4.9)	(2.4)	(49.-)
Tennessee*	(17)	16.1	14.-	13.9	87.1	86.4	99.2	92.4	14.67	11.2	6.8	12.8	87.5	53.-	4.8	2.5	51.3
Arkansas*	(11)	16.65	14.-	13.75	84.3	83.8	99.4	90.9	14.80	11.1	7.1	12.7	88.1	55.8	5.07	2.54	50.2
Louisiana*	(17)	16.86	14.2	14.1	84.3	84.-	99.2	90.9	14.89	11.6	7.04	12.9	89.5	53.4	5.02	2.4	48.-
Florida*	(33)	17.-	14.3	13.6	84.1	80.-	95.1	87.-	14.98	11.9	6.9	13.3	89.5	51.9	5.-	2.4	48.-

*C. I. 80 and above.

Tennessee and Arkansas, however, appear to represent the territorial limits of the type towards the North and Northwest, unless it survives, as seems probable, in some living offshoots such as a part of the Osage and the Winnebago. The eastern states, the Appalachians, the central states and the plains, are occupied by different types of Indians—in larger part by the dolichocephalic to mesocephalic Algonquin, in part by the low-vaulted Sioux and in part by the medium-high old brachycephals of certain portions of the Ohio mound region.

But this is not the whole story. We have roughly traced here the territorial limits of the southern brachycephals, but in all these regions there was a sprinkling also of a high vaulted mesocephalic type of population. This population is plainly not a mere variant of the more round-headed type, and connects with the North. Previous studies on the tribes of the eastern states[1] have shown not only that these tribes as a whole were rather high-vaulted, as is common with the oblong-headed skulls on the whole American continent, but also that as we proceeded southwards the mean height index and also the height-length index were gradually increasing. These records are shown on pages 115, 116.

A study of the Seminole skulls from Florida shows similar features as the West Virginia skulls above—a general relation to the Algonquin type of skull, but often with somewhat increased breadth and generally increased height of the vault; and there are indications that this type was shared more or less by other southeastern oblong-headed people.

It appears that this eastern cranial type, inclining gradually more and more to mesocephaly as well as to a high vault, reached eventually as far south as Florida and as far southwest as Arkan-

---

[1] Bull. 62, B. A. E., 117, 118.

sas and Louisiana. It is according to all indications identical not only with the Seminoles, but evidently also with the older more oblong-headed element of the Floridian population. It is a sub-type which must have belonged to a large portion of the Muskhogeans; and it may be defined as a transitional type between the more northern one of the Algonquins and the Gulf brachycephals.

The Muskhogean confederacy was, according to the evidence we now have at hand, more than a confederacy of blood-related tribes. It was a confederacy of the Seminoles, Creeks, Chicasaws and others whose physical characteristics point more or less to the north, and of the Choctaws, Natchez, Alabamois and related tribes who belonged to a different type of people, to the strong southern brachycephalic stock which included also the bulk of the Floridians.

It would seem from the present facts that the bulk of the Muskhogean people must have been derived originally from the more northern long-headed tribes; that they extended once well towards the south from the Atlantic to and beyond the Mississippi, but did not occupy, or occupied but sparsely or only in spots, the territory along the Gulf; and that then came a relatively strong invasion from the West or Southwest—possibly from Mexico—of people of a distinct type not hitherto represented east of the Mississippi; that this current overflowed the Gulf states and Florida, overcame and absorbed whatever there may have already been there, extended as far as it could northward, and in the course of frequent warfares as well as in amical relations, became extensively mingled and even admixed with the contact tribes, admixing them to a similar extent. The strongest of these contact tribes formed eventually a political union together with the main portion of the southern stock, which union was the Muskhogean confederacy; and they

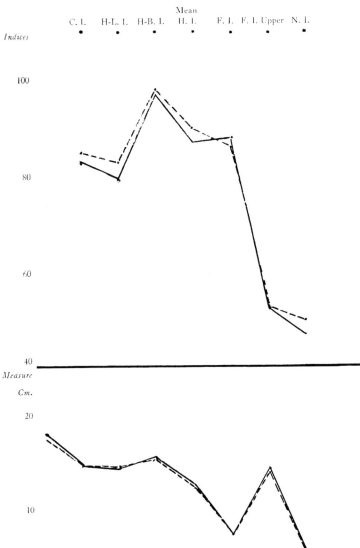

Comparison of Floridian Brachycephals with those
in Neighboring States

Mean

C. I.   H-L. I.   H-B. I.   H. I.   F. I.   F. I. Upper   N. I.

Indices

100

80

60

40
Measure

Cm.

20

10

L   B   H   Cran.   M-N   A. PC.-N   B   H   B
                          Mod.

——————————— Florida   (69 crania)

---------------------- Peri-Floridian (61   "   )

Fig. 6

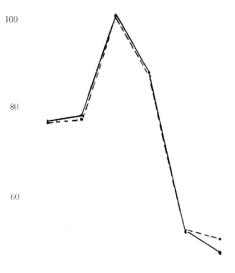

Graphic Comparison of Oblong Crania from
Florida Mounds and Shell Heaps, with those of the Seminoles

Mean

C. I.   H-L. I.   H-B. I.   H. I.   F. I.   N. I.

Indices

100

80

60

40

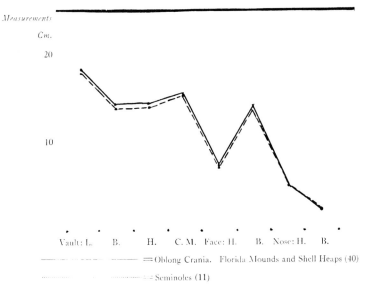

Measurements

Cm.

20

10

Vault: L.   B.   H.   C. M.   Face: H.   B.   Nose: H.   B.

———————————————— = Oblong Crania. Florida Mounds and Shell Heaps (40)

.... = Seminoles (11)

Fig. 7

EASTERN AND SOUTHEASTERN CRANIA: INDIANS

MALES

Locality	Number of Skulls	Cranial Index	Mean Height Index	Height Length Index	Height Breadth Index
Maine	6	72.7	83.-	71.9	98.8
Eastern Canada	14	73.4	84.4	73.1	99.7
New York State	19	73.5	84.4	73.6	99.5
Massachusetts	14	72.8	84.6	73.5	101.-
Rhode Island	6	73.7	85.3	74.1	100.5
Connecticut	4	72.4	86.5	73.5	100.4
Manhattan Island	2	71.7	87.5	75.1	104.8
Long Island	7	70.7	88.1	74.9	105.7
Staten Island	4	71.7	87.5	75.2	104.9
New Jersey (Heye Coll.)	4	73.9	83.9	73.1	98.9
New Jersey (earlier)	6	74.6	86.1	75.8	101.2
Virginia (misc.)	12	75.5	86.5	76.2	99.3
Virginia (western)	15	75.5	89.8	79.-	103.2
Seminoles	11	77.-	87.6	77.6	100.7
Oblong Skulls of Florida	40	77.9	88.1	78.5	100.8

possibly accepted more or less the language or perhaps the main language of the more highly cultured southerners.

This hypothesis would account for the occurrence of oblong heads approaching the Algonquian among the southern tribes, including the older Floridians; it would account for the perceptible dilution of brachycephaly observable in some localities, more particularly in Florida, and it might account for the noticeable broadening and heightening of the skull of these more northern contact tribes, which included particularly the Chicasaws, Creeks and Seminoles.

If these views are correct then, also, the language of those of the Muskhogean tribes who were of northern derivation ought to show traces of the tribes of the North; and one could reasonably doubt the isolation of the Timucuaan.

There are nevertheless other possibilities. One of these is that the Gulf brachycephals represent the original old population of these regions, the oblong heads impinging upon them from the north and penetrating among them later and not accepting, but imparting to them their own language, the Muskhogean. In the latter case it would be the Natchez and Choctaws who ought to show traces of their ancestral tongue, which might not impossibly in such a case be the Timucuaan, whose enigmatic occurrence in a part of the Florida population that we now know was not physically different from the rest, is hard to explain. Linguistics and archeology will doubtless sooner or later throw decisive light on these problems, which from the standpoint of physical anthropology are rather immaterial, for the results in this line remain the same.

Still another view would be that the remarkable height of the skull which is the distinguishing feature of these southern populations, both of the oblong- and of the round-headed kind, is a local or regional development. In general these skulls are all typically and purely Indian, but the accentuated height of at least the rounded skulls is not a generic Indian character and must have developed specially somewhere—why not in the Gulf states? The objections are that in the round-headed type, at least, the feature is universal in the large territory under consideration; that old neighboring people such as the brachy-cephals of Ohio or those of the Antilles, have not been so affected; and that there is not apparent in the great region occupied by these high-skulled people any environmental or other agency sufficiently peculiar or strong or universal to be possibly taken for a cause of such marked physical alteration.

The whole matter shows once more and most strongly the need of our gaining a better knowledge of the anthropology of the eastern parts of Mexico. The head deformation of the Gulf brachycephals, their culture, various elements of their language, all seem to point to Mexico rather than elsewhere; but we have no records, especially no skeletal remains of the eastern Mexican population which would enable us to settle this question definitely one way or the other. The next most pressing need is that of more satisfactory data on the brachycephalic North America Indian population in general and in particular those of the Columbia basin and neighboring regions. Until we have such records we shall be hampered in our generalizations and our work cannot possibly reach the conclusiveness which we strive for.

THE LONG BONES OF FLORIDA

As the object of these studies is not so much a minute de-scription as a broad precision and identification of the remains of the Floridian aborigines, and as in addition our skeletal collections from the peninsula are far from adequate when it comes to many secondary parts of the skeleton, this section will be restricted to the four principal bones of the limbs which are the index of strength and stature, namely, the humerus, radius, femur and tibia.

The specimens included in these examinations are from different parts of Florida, though mainly the west coast, and belonged essentially to the brachycephalic old population. They, as was the case with most of the skulls, show no appreciable differences as to locality and may therefore be legitimately grouped together. The tabulated results which follow are very instructive. They are also quite harmonious.

STATURE OF THE OLD FLORIDA POPULATION

The mean lengths of the four principal long bones, the humerus, radius, femur and tibia, fail to show any exceptional height for the Floridians. The various methods of estimating stature from the lengths of these bones, including the writer's own coefficients obtained on a large amount of dissecting room material, indicate collectively that the mean height of the mound and shell-heap Florida men was between 165 and 168 cm. (approximately 5 ft. 6 in.), while that of the women was between 152 and 154 cm. (about 5 ft.)—which is very near the averages of our present mixed white population. The tallest Florida male represented in our collection reached not over 178 cm., or 5 ft. 10 in. Thus ends the fallacy of the "giant-like" Floridians, inspired probably by their sturdy build, by the apprehension of the Spaniards who first came into contact with them, and by their comparing them with the smaller Indians they knew before as well as with themselves.

THE HUMERUS

The following two tables give the dimensions of the Florida humerus. The length of the female bones to that of the males is as 91 to 100, compared to 91.2 among North American Indians in general—a remarkable uniformity. Similar relations as to strength of shaft at middle are 85 in the Floridians, 91.3 among

FLORIDA—HUMERUS

| | Length | At Middle: | | | |
		D. Max.	D. Min.	Mean Diam.	Index
	cm.	cm.	cm.	cm.	
BOTH SIDES					
Males	(18)	(40)	(40)	(40)	(40)
Aver.	32.3	2.41	1.84	2.13	**76.5**
Min.	29.3	2.1	1.65	1.90	69.1
Max.	34.5	2.95	2.2	2.57	91.5
Females	(8)	(45)	(45)	(45)	(45)
Aver.	29.4	2.10	1.53	1.81	**72.8**
Min.	27.8	1.7	1.30	1.5	61.9
Max.	31.–	2.4	1.85	2.1	83.–
RIGHT					
Males	(13)	(20)	(20)	(20)	(20)
Aver.	32.72	2.47	1.86	2.165	*75.1*
Females	(5)	(22)	(22)	(22)	(22)
Aver.	29.32	2.11	1.49	1.80	*70.9*
LEFT					
Males	(5)	(20)	(20)	(20)	(20)
Aver.	31.52	2.35	1.83	2.09	*77.9*
Females	(3)	(23)	(23)	(23)	(23)
Aver.	29.47	2.09	1.56	1.825	*74.6*

FLORIDA HUMERI, CONTRASTED WITH THOSE OF OTHER N. A. INDIANS AND U. S. WHITES

	Number of Specimens		Length Maximum		Dimensions at Middle of Shaft:									
					Number of Specimens		Diameter Major		Diameter Minor		Mean Diameter		Index of Shaft	
	Male	Female	Male	Female	Male	Female	Male	Female	Male	Female	Male	Female	Male	Female
			cm.	cm.			cm.	cm.	cm.	cm.	cm.	cm.		
Florida	(18)	(8)	32.3	29.4	(40)	(45)	2.41	2.10	1.84	1.53	2.13	1.81	76.5	72.8
North American Indians in General	(378)	(262)	31.8	28.9	(478)	(356)	2.22	2.–	1.63	1.40	1.93	1.70	73.1	70.2
U. S. Whites (All Nationalities)	(1930)	(770)	32.5	29.8	(1930)	(770)	2.26	2.04	1.87	1.62	2.07	1.83	83.–	79.3

Indians in general, 91.6 in American whites. The sexual difference in the Florida humeri is here relatively large, which as
will be seen later is due to an excess of strength of the bone
in the males of the peninsula. The right bone is notably stronger
than the left in breadth and somewhat stronger also in thickness
in the males; the right is slightly the broader, but the left slightly
thicker than the right in the females, pointing to marked differences in occupation of the two sexes.

The second table shows the Florida humeri to be slightly
longer than the average in all our other available Indian series,
and almost exactly like those of the actual mixed white population of the United States. In robustness they exceed in both
dimensions and both sexes, but more particularly in the males, the
general average of the Indians. In the males they, in fact, exceed
slightly even the ordinary American whites, the females in the
two groups being very nearly alike with the figures very slightly
in favor of the working white woman. The mean strength of
the male bones compares with that of North American Indians
in general as 111.5, that of the female as 107.1 to 100. It was
doubtless their strenuous life as boatmen and fishermen that
accounts for this extraordinary strength of the arm of the male
Floridian.

In accord with its strength, the index of the shaft at middle
is in both sexes higher—in other words, the humerus is less flat—
than in the average Indian, but is still very perceptibly lower
than in whites. This flatness of the humerus, together with that
of the tibia and the subtrochanteric portion of the femur, is
a generalized racial characteristic of the American Indian.

Perforation of the Septum.—The 48 male humeri that could
be examined for this feature give 22.1 per cent., the 30 female
bones, 70 per cent. of perforations. This gives the mean of 46.5
per cent., which is considerably higher than that in Indians in

general (30 per cent. in 2,985 bones) and of course very much higher than in other races (U. S. Whites 5.3 per cent., U. S. Negroes 19 per cent.). It is also the maximum for any tribe thus far examined except, which is interesting, the Indians of Arkansas and Louisiana (46 per cent. of perforations), who, as we have seen in connection with the skull, belonged to the same stock as the Floridians.

More in detail the conditions found were as follows:

FLORIDA HUMERI: PERFORATION OF SEPTUM

Sex and Number of Specimens	Perforations pp. (pin-point)	1 (small)	2 (medium)	3 (large)	All
	Per cent.	Per cent.	Per cent.	Per cent.	Per cent.
Males (48)	2.1	14.6	4.2	2.1	23
Females (30)	3.3	40.-	23.3	3.3	70

Supracondyloid Process.—This atavistic process occurring in about 1 per cent. of the arm bones of whites,[1] but very rare as a distinct process in Indians in general, forms no exception in this respect in the Floridians. It was present as a definite projection in none of the bones, the conditions being found as shown herewith:

FLORIDA HUMERI: SUPRACONDYLOID PROCESS

Sex and Number of Specimens	Rough Trace in its Place	Slight Ridge	Moderate Ridge	Pronounced Ridge	Tubercle, Spine or Process
	Per cent.	Per cent.	Per cent.	Per cent.	Per cent..
Males (48)	6.3	14.6	4.2	. . . .	. . . .
Females (41)	. . .	2.4	. . . . . .	. . . .	. . . .

THE RADIUS

While there were in the collections examined numerous more or less imperfect Florida radii that showed well the general

---

[1] See Terry (R. J.). Am. J. Phys. Anthrop., 1921, iv, 129.

characteristics of the bone—which did not present anything extraordinary—there were found but 14 specimens that could be measured for length. Eleven of these, identified as male, gave the mean length of 24.6 (23.2–25.6) cm., 3 identified as female, 23.7 (23.1–24.9) cm. All the bones seen were of good strength, with moderate curve.

The radio-humeral index $\frac{R \times 100}{H}$, based on the above measurements and on the mean length of the humeri is, in the males, 76. 2, which is very close to the general North American Indian average of 77.7. In mixed American whites (526 skeletons) the writer obtained the average radiohumeral index of 73.6. The Indian radius, and hence forearm, as that of the negro (R–H. I. in males 77.4), is relatively long—another racial feature of import that in advanced tasks of the anthropology of both the yellow-brown and the white race should prove of much assistance.

THE FEMUR

There were found 28 old Floridian femora that were sufficiently preserved to give the standard bicondylar length, but in 128 bones it was possible to measure the thickness of the median part of the shaft. The length shows that the bones while not short, are of no great size. The female is to the male femur in this respect as 92.5 to 100—practically the same as in other Indians (92.65), but less than in United States whites (93.–) or negroes (93.1). The right bone is on the average slightly the longer in both sexes. The range of variation is moderate.

A reference to the accompanying tables shows the Florida femur to be perceptibly longer than the mean of all available tribes, but slightly shorter than that of the mixed present white American population.

In strength the Florida femur shows well above the general Indian average in the males and slightly above also in the females. Exactly the same will be seen with the tibia. In both cases the excess of the female bone over the general Indian average is less than with the humerus, showing probably the effects of canoe life in the Floridians. Take away the canoe and the Florida woman would presumably be of the same strength, indicating the same activities, as her Indian sisters in general—not quite on the whole reaching the mean robustness of the working female white American. The Florida male excels in strength throughout, in upper as well as lower extremities. He was evidently both well nourished and very active as well on land as on water.

The form of the Florida femur as expressed by the shaft index at the middle of the bone $\frac{(\text{Diam. later. max.} \times 100)}{(\text{Diam. antero-post.})}$ is, as may be seen in the following tables, the same as in Indians at large, and is in all the tribes notably lower than in whites. This is due to the relatively as well as absolutely greater breadth (Diam. lat. max.) of the bone in the whites, while in the Indian and particularly the Florida males it is associated with a greater antero-posterior diameter—features constituting further racial differences of real value.

The humero-femoral index $\frac{(\text{H} \times 100)}{(\text{Bicond. L. of F.})}$ is approximately 73.1 in the males and 71.9 in the females; in 150 male and 100 female Indians (500 femora) of other tribes the index was respectively 72.2 and 72.5; in 400 male and 145 female U. S. whites it was 72.5 and 71.6. The index evidently differs but little either tribally or racially, nevertheless it inclines to be slightly higher in the Indians, denoting a slightly shorter relative length of the femur.

FLORIDA—FEMUR					
	Length Bicondylar cm.	At Middle:			
		D. A-P. Max. cm.	D. Later. cm.	Mean Diam. cm.	Index
BOTH SIDES					
Males	(20)	(86)	(86)	(86)	(86)
Aver.	44.2	3.09	2.72	2.91	87.9
Min.	41.8	2.7	2.3	2.55	74.3
Max.	47.9	3.5	3.3	3.3	100.-
Females	(8)	(36)	(36)	(36)	(36)
Aver.	40.9	2.61	2.36	2.49	90.3
Min.	38.3	2.4	2.1	2.27	78.6
Max.	44.8	2.9	2.6	2.65	100.-
RIGHT					
Males	(8)	(42)	(42)	(42)	(42)
Aver.	44.3	3.11	2.72	2.92	87.5
Females	(4)	(19)	(19)	(19)	(19)
Aver.	41.3	2.65	2.32	2.48	87.7
LEFT					
Males	(12)	(44)	(44)	(44)	(44)
Aver.	44.1	3.08	2.72	2.90	88.3
Females	(4)	(17)	(17)	(17)	(17)
Aver.	40.6	2.57	2.40	2.49	93.3

Florida Femora, Contrasted with Those of Other N. A. Indians and U. S. Whites

| | Number of Specimens | | Biocondylar Length | | Dimensions at Middle of Shaft: | | | | | | | | | | |
| | | | | | Number of Specimens | | Diam. Ant.-Post. Max. | | Diameter Lateral | | Mean Diameter | | Index of Shaft | |
	Male	Female	Male	Female	Male	Female	Male	Female	Male	Female	Male	Female	Male	Female
			cm.	*cm.*			*cm.*	*cm.*	*cm.*	*cm.*	*cm.*	*cm.*		
Florida	(20)	(8)	44.2	40.9	(86)	(36)	3.09	2.61	2.72	2.36	2.91	2.49	87.9	90.3
North American Indians in General	(902)	(327)	42.7	40.3	(522)	(330)	2.95	2.57	2.58	2.36	2.77	2.47	87.3	91.8
U. S. Whites	(207)	(100)	44.9	41.9	(207)	(100)	2.93	2.65	2.85	2.60	2.89	2.62	97.–	98.2

THE TIBIA

In agreement with the humeri and femora, the Florida tibiæ show but medium length.   The female to male average is as 91.3 to 100; in 1130 tibiæ of other tribes it averages 91.8; in 2000 bones of mixed U. S. whites 92.7 to 100.   The right Floridian tibia appears on the average as slightly the longer in both sexes, which is rather exceptional, in many Indian as well as other racial groups the left tibia, in one of the sexes at least, being the longer.

The tibio-femoral index $\dfrac{(T \times 100)}{(\text{Bicond. L. of F.})}$ equals 83.− in the males and 81.9 in the females, which is about two points less than in the Indians at large, though still slightly higher than in whites (male whites 82.1, females 81.5).   It is interesting to note that there should be so much less racial difference between the leg and the thigh than between the forearm and arm.

The strength of the bone is marked.   It is equal on the two sides in the males, slightly greater on the left in the females. The average male bone is in this respect to the average female bone as 83.3 to 100, which is approximately two points lower than the general average of other tribes (7 tribes = 85.5), showing the male Florida tibia to be exceptionally strong, which stands in accord to what was observed with the rest of the long bones from the peninsula.

Comparison with other tribes as given in the second table below shows that, while the female Florida tibia is just about or only very slightly above the general Indian average, and with this slightly below that of the working classes of mixed U. S. whites, the male bone is well above the average of the Indian as well as that of the common male whites.   The Florida males, to sum up, may therefore well be characterized as decidedly robust.   They were not giants in stature, but were strong in frame and musculature.   It can readily be understood that they had the reputation of fierce fighters.

FLORIDA—TIBIA				
Length (Intern. Agr.) cm.	At Middle:			
	D.-A.-P. Max. cm.	D. Lateral cm.	Mean Diam. cm.	Index
BOTH SIDES				
Males (12)	(56)	(56)	(56)	(56)
Aver. 36.7	3.37	2.25	2.81	66.6
Min. 35.8	2.9	1.85	2.45	56.1
Max. 37.8	3.8	2.6	3.1	80.–
Females (10)	(55)	(55)	(55)	(55)
Aver. 33.5	2.77	1.92	2.34	69.2
Min. 30.4	2.35	1.6	2.02	55.–
Max. 36.5	3.3	2.25	2.72	78.6
RIGHT				
Males (5)	(25)	(25)	(25)	(25)
Aver. 35.14	3.35	2.26	2.81	67.4
Females (5)	(22)	(22)	(22)	(22)
Aver. 33.6	2.73	1.92	2.32	70.1
LEFT				
Males (7)	(31)	(31)	(31)	(31)
Aver. 36.96	3.39	2.23	2.81	65.7
Females (5)	(33)	(33)	(33)	(33)
Aver. 33.92	2.81	1.92	2.37	68.4

FLORIDA TIBIÆ, CONTRASTED WITH THOSE OF OTHER N. A. INDIANS AND U. S. WHITES	Number of Specimens		Length (Geneva Agr.)		Dimensions at Middle of Shaft:								
					Number of Specimens		Diam. Ant.-post. max.		Diam. Lateral		Mean Diam.		Index of Shaft.
	Male	Female	Male	Female	Male	Female	Male	Female	Male	Female	Male	Female	Male	Female
			cm.	*cm.*			*cm.*	*cm.*	*cm.*	*cm.*	*cm.*	*cm.*		
Florida	(12)	(9)	36.7	34.2	(56)	(55)	3.37	2.77	2.25	1.92	2.81	2.34	66.5	69.2
North American Indians in General	(324)	(214)	36.9	34.1	(362)	(243)	3.28	2.74	2.16	1.93	2.72	2.33	65.8	70.5
U. S. Whites (All Nationalities)	(1638)	(814)	36.3	33.7	(1165)	(575)	3.11	2.75	2.26	2.03	2.68	2.39	72.7	73.8

In observing the separate measurements of the shaft of the tibia it will be noted that the plus development of the Florida bone in relation to that of other Indians is in both dimensions, in relation to whites only in the antero-posterior diameter. This means a bone giving very nearly the same index of shaft or same degree of platycnæmy as that of Indians in general, but a very perceptibly lower index or higher platycnæmy than that of whites. An antero-posteriorly deeper and therefore relatively flatter femur, an antero-posteriorly larger and therefore also relatively flatter tibia—such in comparison with whites (and especially negroes) are the essential Indian and equally Floridian characteristics in these important parts of the skeleton.

SUMMARY OF THE OBSERVATIONS ON THE SKELETAL REMAINS
FROM THE FLORIDA MOUNDS AND SHELL HEAPS

1. The skeletal remains from the mounds and shell heaps of Florida show considerable uniformity; yet it is possible to distinguish two types—one prevalent, fundamental, characterized by above-average massiveness, brachycephaly, and high vault of skull, high, fairly broad face, high, moderately broad nose, and high, stout lower jaw, with robust to heavy, good-sized skeleton; and another, less numerous and in the main evidently more recent type, with head form subdolicho- to slightly brachycephalic, also high-vaulted, and with facial and skeletal features related to but somewhat less accentuated than those of the first type.

2. The first type not seldom exists pure, the second is most frequently admixed with the first. There are no traces of any other type in the territory.

3. The brachycephals extended in the main over the northern two-thirds of the peninsula, the oblong heads being more frequent in the southern third and along parts of the east coast. The Timucuas of northern Florida, the St. John's River Indians, and

the Caloosas of the west coast or at least those from Tampa Bay to Charlotte Harbor, were all physically the same people.

4. The brachycephals practiced the fronto-occipital artificial deformation of the head; the oblong heads, except where admixed with the brachycephals, practiced no deformation.

5. The physical affinities of the brachycephalic population of Florida lie not to the south, but to the immediate north and west. They are clearly identifiable as an extension of a large block of people of the same type who occupied at and before the time of discovery large portions of the states of Arkansas, Louisiana, Mississippi, Tennessee, Alabama, Georgia and probably also South Carolina.

6. This stock has no affinities towards the northeast or north, and must have been derived from somewhere in the northwest, west or southwest. For the present, indications would seem to favor eastern Mexico.

7. Since discovery the type, though robust, and strong in numbers, has become very largely extinct except in the mixed survivors of the Choctaw. Tribes that may be offshoots of this body, though now speaking northern languages, are one part of the Osage and the Winnebago.

8. The more oblong-headed elements of Florida may be safely identified with the Seminoles and other Muskhogean tribes of northern derivation.

9. The study of the long bones of the Florida brachycephals shows an exceptional robustness and strength for the males; otherwise they closely agree in every respect with the means of North American Indians in general.

10. Estimations of stature from the long bones show the same height as the present mixed (not Old American) United States population.

In order further to clear the anthropological problem of the Floridian peninsula and of the south in general, it is highly desirable that more skeletal material be collected from the eastern as well as the western coast regions, from the latitude of Lake Okechobee and Charlotte Harbour southward. More material of the same nature is also needed from the Carolinas, northern Georgia and western Texas. And an effort should be made to locate and make anthropometric observations on the possible remaining full-bloods of the Yamasees, Uchees, Creeks, Chickasaws and other tribes that once belonged to the general region under consideration. With this comparatively modest amount of additional work we shall have covered a large and important part of the northern continent, and established a firm foundation for future comparison and deductions.

DETAILED MEASUREMENTS

FLORIDA CRANIA (ALL)

MALES

Place	Coll.	No.	Locality	Deformation	Special	Vault: L.	B.	H. (Bas-Bg.)	C.I.	H.L.I.	H.B.I.	Mean H.I.	Cranial Module	Face: Ment-Nas.	Alv. Pt.-Nas.	D. bizyg. max.	F.I. total	F.I. upper	Nose: L.	B.	N.I.
WEST COAST	U.S.N.M.	242,630	PENSACOLA BAY	sl. later. occip. flat.	—	18.8	15.4	—	81.9	83.–	102.–	91.6	15.60	12.9	8.1	14.3	90.2	56.6	5.5	2.4	46.4
		242,631	"	—	—	17.7	14.4	14.7	81.4	80.1	108.8	92.3	15.73		7.7	13.6	(111.–)	(65.4)	5.6	2.7	48.2
		242,665	"	mod. occip. flat.	—	18.6	13.7	14.9	73.7				15.60	(15.1)	(8.9)	13.1	94.7	61.1	(6.–)	(2.15)	(35.8)
		242,632	"	pron. occip. flat.	—	(16.7)	(15.3)	(14.8)					14.87	12.4	8.–				5.3	2.65	50.–
		242,668	"	pron. occip. flat.	—	(16.2)	(14.4)	(14.–)					16.23								
		242,670	"		—	(18.3)	(15.6)	(14.8)													
	A.N.S.P.	2194,	ST. ANDREWS BAY Pierce Md.	mod. fr. flat. (meas's O.K.)	—	18.1	14.7	13.8	81.2	76.2	93.9	84.2	15.53		7.3	14.2		51.4	5.2	2.3	44.2
		2,188	n. APALACHICOLA	—	—	17.2	14.–	13.6	81.4	79.1	97.1	87.2	14.93		6.6	13.8		47.8	4.6	2.6	56.5
		2,196	JIGGER POINT	—	—	16.8	14.4	13.8	85.7	82.1	95.8	88.5	15.–		6.9	13.8		50.–	4.6	2.4	52.2
		2,197	(n. Cedar Keyes) Levy Co.	—	v.	16.5	13.6	13.6	82.4	82.4	100.–	90.4	14.57		7.3	14.–		52.1	5.3	2.5	47.2
		2,198	"	—	v. heavy	17.8	14.8	14.4	83.2	80.9	97.3	88.3	15.67		7.3	14.6		50.–	5.5	2.65	48.2
		2,199	"	—	—	17.5	13.8	14.3	78.9	81.7	103.6	91.4	15.20			13.4			(3.1)	2.1	(67.7)
		2,200	"	—	—	18.9	14.–	14.–	77.8	77.8	100.–	87.5	15.33		6.8	14.3		47.6	4.9	2.55	52.–
		2,202	"	sl. fr-occ. flat.	—	18.–	14.–	14.1	77.8	77.7	97.9	87.9	15.40		7.6	13.8		55.1	5.–	2.45	49.–
		2,203	"	—	—	18.1	15.–	14.4	82.9	79.6	96.–	87.6	15.83	12.7	7.6	14.8	85.8	51.4	5.5	2.8	50.9
		2,204	"	—	—																
	U.S.N.M.	2,205	CEDAR KEYES	—	—	18.4	14.2	14.–	77.2	76.1	98.6	85.9	15.53		7.–	14.7		47.6	4.8	2.2	45.8
		227,499	"	—	—	17.6	14.–	13.7	76.6	77.8	97.9	86.7	15.10		7.–	14.2		40.3	5.1	2.5	49.–
		16,533	"	sl. occ. flat.	—	18.9	14.5	14.2	76.7	75.1	97.9	85.–	15.87		8.4	15.2		55.3	5.3	2.65	50.–
		16,332	"	—	—	17.5	14.7		84.–		94.–	86.1	15.73								
	W.I.	15,481	SAFFORD MD. Tarpon Springs Hillsboro Co.	—	—	17.9	15.1	14.3	84.4	79.3	94.–	86.1	15.77		8.4						
		15,485	"	—	—	18.–	14.6	13.9	81.1	77.2	95.2	85.3	15.50								
		15,782	"	sl. fr-occ. flat.	—	18.1	14.2	14.–	78.4	77.4	96.7	85.3	15.43								
		15,788	"	—	—	17.8	14.3	14.1	80.3	79.2	98.6	87.8	15.40								
		15,790	"	sl. front. flat.	—	18.–	15.7		87.2												
		15,791	"	—	—	18.5	14.8	14.2	80.–	76.8	96.–	85.3	15.83								
		15,844	"	sl. occ. flat.	—	17.9	15.1	14.6	84.4	81.6	95.7	88.5	15.87								
		15,849	"	—	—	18.4	15.–	14.4	80.4	78.3	96.8	86.8	15.87								
		15,852	"	sl. fr-occ. flat.	—	18.4	15.–	13.8	81.5	75.–	92.–	82.6	15.73								
		15,853	"	—	—	18.4	15.–	14.–	79.9	76.1	84.6	84.6	15.70						5.2	2.45	47.1
		15,855	"	—	—	17.6	14.7	14.–	83.5	79.6	95.2	86.7	15.43		7.7	14.1		51.8	5.1	2.6	51.–
		15,856	"	—	—	17.8	14.9	13.6	83.7	76.4	91.3	83.2	15.43		8.1				5.8	2.7	46.6

Place:	Coll.	No.	Locality	Deformation	Special	Vault: L.	B.	H. (Bas-Bg.)	C.I.	H.L.I.	H.B.I.	Mean H.I.	Cranial Mod. ulc	Face: Ment. Nas.	Alv. Pt. Nas.	D. bizyg. max.	F.I. total	F.I. upper	Nose: L.	B.	N.I.
WEST COAST	W.I.	15,858	Clearwater, n. Tampa			17.4	14.6		83.9												
		15,854	"			18.4	14.6	14.7	79.4		100.7	89.1	15.90			? 14.6					
		15,958	"			17.4	14.6		83.9												
		15,961	"			18.6	15.5		83.3												
		16,001	"		thick	18.5	14.8		80.–												
		16,007	"			18.4	14.7	14.2	79.9	79.9					7.8			53.4	5.3	2.3	43.4
		16,012	"			18.2	14.6		80.2												
		16,099	"			18.8	14.4		76.6	78.–	97.3	86.6	15.67								
	U.S. N. M.	243,691	"			18.2	14.8	14.–	81.3	76.9	94.6	84.8	15.73	12.7	7.8				5.5	2.55	46.4
		243,693	"	sl. occ. flat.		18.6	15.–		80.6												
		243,695	"			17.6	14.7														
		243,696	"			18.4	14.4		78.3					12.9							
	A.N.S.P.	2,206	Hog Id., off Tampa Bay			17.8	14.4	14.–	80.9	78.6	97.2	87.–	15.40		7.8	14.4	91.4	54.2	5.4	2.5	46.3
		2,207	"			17.7	14.–	13.8	79.1	78.–	98.6	87.1	15.17			13.9		56.1	5.4	2.7	50.–
		2,208	"			17.2	14.–	13.6	81.4	79.1	97.1	87.2	14.93		7.2	13.5		55.3	5.1	2.3	45.1
		2,209	"			17.6	14.2	14.2	80.7	80.7	100.–	89.3	15.33			14.1	91.5	55.1	5.3	2.3	43.4
		22,020	"			17.7	14.–	14.2	79.1	80.2	101.4	89.6	15.30	12.9	6.6	13.9		47.5	4.9	2.6	53.1
		22,021	"	sl. asym.		17.7	14.4		81.4	81.9	100.7	90.3	15.53		7.8	13.7	94.2	56.9	5.7	2.5	43.9
		22,022	"			17.7	14.4	14.5	79.1	81.9	103.5	91.4	15.83		8.1	14.8		54.7	5.7	2.2	38.6
		22,023	"			18.2	13.7	14.9	80.6	85.3	95.6	85.3	14.60		7.6	13.2		57.6	5.3	2.35	44.3
		22,024	"			17.8	14.1	13.1	79.2	78.6	99.3	87.8	15.30		7.6	13.7		55.5	5.6	2.4	42.9
		2,211	Johns Pass, Tampa Bay		atypical	19.1	14.6	14.–	76.4	74.4	97.3	84.3	15.97	11.7	7.–	14.7	79.6	47.6	4.9	2.7	55.1
		2,212	"			18.–	14.6	14.2	81.1	80.–	98.6	88.3	15.67		7.5	14.2		52.8	5.6	2.3	41.1
		2,216	"			17.1	13.4	14.4	78.4	79.5	101.5	88.2	14.70		7.4	13.0		53.2	5.1	2.3	45.1
		2,217	"			17.–	13.7	13.6	80.6	81.2	100.7	89.9	14.83		7.4	13.4		55.2	4.9	2.2	44.9
		2,219	"		sm. atypical sl. asym.	17.6	13.6	13.8	77.3	77.3	100.–	87.2	14.93		7.–	13.7		51.1	4.9	2.4	49.–
	U.S. N. M.	242,653	Tampa Bay			18.1	13.6	13.6	75.1	80.7	107.3	92.1	15.43	12.2	7.9				5.9	2.7	45.8
		242,651	"	or v. sl. occ. fl.		19.3	14.7	14.6	76.2												
		242,640	"			18.8	14.4	14.4	76.6						7.4				5.2	2.6	50.–
		242,652	"			17.7	14.–	15.–	79.1	84.7	107.1	94.6	15.57	12.5		14.4	86.8	54.2	5.4	2.6	48.1
		242,620	"			18.3	14.5	14.5	79.2	81.4	101.4	90.3	15.97		7.8						
		292,775	"			18.3	14.7	11.9	80.3	81.1	90.3	89.3	15.77						5.3	2.5	47.2
		292,776	"			19.3	15.7		81.3												
		242,639	"	sl. lat. occ. flat.		18.–	14.–	14.6	81.7	81.1	99.3	90.3			7.1						
		242,671	"			17.4	14.3		82.2												
		242,635	"			17.8	14.7		82.6												47.2
		242,682	"	mod. occ. flat.		17.7	14.9		84.2												
		242,613	"			18.–	16.–		89.9												
		212,610	Anclote Riv.			16.–									8.–				5.5	2.9	52.7
		212,684	"			18.2	14.7	14.7	80.8		100.–	92.2	15.87						5.4	2.5	46.3

FLORIDA CRANIA (ALL)

MALES

Place	No.	Locality	Deformation	Special	Vault: L.	B.	H. (Bas-Bg.)	C.I.	H.L.I.	H.B.I.	Mean H.I.	Cran. Module	Face: Ment.-Nas.	Alv. Pt.-Nas.	D. bizyg. max.	F.I. total	F.I. upper	Nose: L.	B.	N.I.
WEST COAST (Cont.) U.S.N.M.	306,701	Manatee	—	—	18.2	14.9	14.4	81.9	79.1	96.6	87.-	15.83	12.3	7.7	14.9	82.6	51.7	5.8	2.6	44.7
	225,075	Sarasota Bay	—	—	17.9	15.6	13.7	87.1	76.5	87.8	81.8	15.73	—	7.5	14.5	—	51.7	5.4	2.5	46.3
	300,118	Charlotte Bay	—	—	18.5	14.8	13.6	80.-	73.5	91.9	81.7	15.63	—	—	14.8	—	—	5.6	2.7	48.2
	315,004	and Fort Myers	—	—	17.9	13.9	14.3	77.6	79.9	102.9	89.9	15.37	—	7.8	13.9	—	56.1	5.7	2.4	42.1
	292,753	"	possibly sl. fr.-occ. flat.	—	17.2	14.-	—	81.4	—	—	—	—	13.-	7.7	14.1	—	54.6	5.4	2.4	44.4
W.I.	15,477	"	flat.	—	19.-	—	—	77.0	—	—	—	—	—	—	—	—	—	—	—	—
	15,487	"	—	—	18.4	14.7	—	77.9	—	—	—	—	—	—	—	—	—	—	—	—
A.N.S.P.	2,228	"	—	—	17.8	14.5	14.4	81.5	80.9	99.3	90.3	15.57	—	7.6	14.5	—	52.4	5.3	2.5	47.2
	2,229	"	—	—	17.6	14.4	14.-	81.8	79.6	97.2	87.5	15.33	—	6.8	13.7	—	49.6	4.8	2.3	47.9
	2,230	"	—	—	18.-	14.5	14.2	80.6	78.9	97.9	87.4	15.57	—	n. 6.8	13.3	—	51.1	4.8	2.7	56.2
MEANS, WEST COAST:					(78) 17.59	(78) 14.53	(55) 14.14	(55) 80.8	(55) 79.-	(55) 98.2	(55) 87.6	(55) 15.48	(11) 12.56	(44) 7.47	(40) 14.09	(10) 88.9	(37) 52.6	(47) 5.29	(47) 2.5	(47) 47.3
ST. JOHNS RIVER A.N.S.P.	1,809	St. Johns River Huntoon Id.	—	—	18.2	14.-	m. 14.1	76.0	71.5	100.7	87.6	15.77	—	—	—	—	—	—	—	—
	1,804		—	—	17.2	13.9	—	80.8	—	—	—	—	—	—	—	—	—	—	—	—
	1,805		—	—	17.8	14.5	—	81.5	—	—	—	—	—	—	15.1	—	47.7	5.2	2.4	46.2
	1,807		—	—	17.7	14.5	—	81.9	—	—	—	—	—	—	15.-	—	47.3	5.-	2.3	46.-
	1,781	Thursby Md.	—	—	18.2	14.7	13.7	80.8	75.3	93.2	83.3	15.53	—	7.2	—	—	—	—	—	—
	1,782	Thursby Md.	sl. front. flat.	—	18.1	14.9	14.5	82.3	80.1	97.3	87.9	15.83	—	7.1	—	—	—	—	—	—
	1,785	Duval's Ldg.	—	—	17.8	14.7	—	81.5	—	—	—	—	—	7.5	n. 15.4	n. 86.4	48.7	4.9	2.4	49.-
	1,784	Ginn's Grove	sl. front. flat.	—	18.6	15.6	14.6	83.0	80.7	95.4	87.4	16.-	n. 13.3	—	—	—	—	—	—	—
	1,796	Tick Id.	—	—	18.1	15.3	—	82.6	—	—	—	—	—	—	—	—	—	—	—	—
	1,797	Sand Md.	—	—	17.8	14.7	—	82.6	—	—	—	—	—	—	—	—	—	—	—	—
	1,792		—	syph.	17.3	15.-	13.8	86.7	79.8	92.-	85.4	15.37	—	—	—	—	—	—	—	—
	1,803	L. Harney	—	—	18.8	14.6	14.6	77.7	77.7	100.-	87.4	16.-	—	—	—	—	—	5.5	2.35	42.7
	1,802	"	—	—	18.1	14.8	14.3	81.8	77.0	96.6	86.9	15.73	—	7.9	14.6	—	54.1	5.4	—	—
	1,810	"	—	—	17.8	14.6	14.-	82.-	78.6	95.9	86.4	15.47	—	—	14.5	—	—	5.4	—	—
	1,790		—	—	18.3 m.	m. 15.-	—	82.-	—	—	—	—	—	—	—	—	—	—	—	—
	1,811	Mulberry Md.	—	—	17.6	15.3	15.3	86.9	—	—	—	—	—	—	—	—	—	—	—	—
MEANS, ST. JOHNS RIVER:					(16) 17.96	(16) 14.75	(8) 14.2	(16) 81.5	(8) 78.6	(8) 96.4	(8) 86.6	(8) 15.67		(4) 7.4	(5) 14.9	(4) 49.5		(6) 5.2	(4) 2.35	(4) 45.9

Place	No.	Locality	Deformation	Special	Vault L.	B.	H. (Bas-Bg.)	C.I.	H.L. I.	H.B. I.	Mean H.I.	Cranial Module	Ment.-Nas.	Alv.-Pt.-Nas.	D. bizyg. max.	F.I. total	F.I. upper	Nose L.	B.	N.I.
EAST COAST AND INLAND U.S.N.M.	242,662	Amelia Id.	—	—	18.4	14.2	14.3	77.2	77.7	100.7	87.7	15.63	11.8	7.4	12.7	—	—	5.2	2.2	42.3
	178,813	St. Augustine	—	—	18.8	14.4	13.3	76.6	70.7	92.4	80.1	15.50	—	6.9	—	—	54.3	4.9	2.2	44.9
	242,664	Gainsville	—	—	18.1	14.4	—	76.6	—	—	—	—	—	—	—	—	—	5.-	—	46.-
	242,683	New Smyrna	—	—	17.8	14.5	14.5	81.5	81.5	100.-	89.8	15.60	—	—	—	—	—	5.-	2.3	—
	242,625	"	—	—	18.6	14.3	14.2	77.4	76.3	98.6	86.1	15.73	—	—	—	—	—	—	—	—
	242,622	"	—	—	17.3	13.5	14.1	78.-	81.5	107.6	91.6	14.97	—	—	—	—	—	5.3	2.5	47.2
	242,619	"	—	sl. asym.	17.2	14.2	13.8	82.6	80.2	97.2	87.9	15.07	—	—	13.8	—	—	—	—	—
	242,624	Maxime Cr.	—	—	17.6	14.6	13.8	83.-	78.4	94.5	85.7	15.33	n.11.7	7.6	n.14.2	82.4	—	5.5	2.5	45.4
	242,629	"	—	—	18.8	14.9	14.4	79.3	76.6	96.6	85.5	16.03	—	—	15.1	—	—	5.3	3.-	56.6
	242,621	Indian River	—	—	19.-	15.4	15.-	81.-	79.-	97.4	87.2	16.47	—	—	—	—	—	5.4	2.85	52.8
	292,778	N. Vero	—	—	17.4	14.4	14.8	82.8	85.1	102.8	93.1	15.53	12.6	7.9	14.1	89.4	56.-	5.6	2.8	50.-
MEANS, EAST COAST:					(11) 18.00	(11) 14.44	(10) 14.22	(11) 79.8	(10) 78.6	(10) 98.4	(10) 87.4	(10) 15.59	(3) 12.-	(4) 7.45	(5) 14.-	(2) 85.9	(2) 55.1	(8) 5.3	(8) 2.55	(8) 48.2
SOUTH AND S.E. FLORIDA U.S.N.M.	228,338	Lake Okechobee	—	—	17.6	13.2	(high)	75.-	78.-	102.2	85.8	15.77	12.2	—	14.6	83.6	—	4.8	2.4	50.-
	228,451	"	—	—	18.2	13.9	14.2	76.4	80.-	103.7	90.3	15.-	13.-	7.7	13.8	94.2	55.8	5.5	2.5	45.4
	243,688	"	—	—	17.5	13.5	14.-	77.1	83.3	106.9	93.6	16.20	11.4	—	13.1	87.-	—	4.9	2.5	51.-
	228,462	Miami	—	—	18.6	14.5	15.5	78.-	—	—	—	—	12.7	7.4	14.-	86.4	52.9	5.3	2.45	46.2
	228,487	So. Fla.	—	—	18.5	14.7	—	79.5	—	—	—	—	—	—	—	—	—	—	—	—
MEANS, SOUTH AND S. E. FLORIDA:					(5) 18.08	(5) 13.96	(3) 14.56	(5) 77.2	(3) 80.5	(3) 104.3	(3) 90.9	(3) 15.54	(4) 12.3	(2) 7.55	(4) 13.9	(4) 88.8	(4) 54.4	(4) 5.1	(4) 2.46	(4) 48.-
SEMINOLES A.N.S.P.	1,286	Various (all fresh or nearly so)	—	small, but male	17.2	12.7	13.8	73.8	80.2	108.7	92.3	14.57	11.8	6.8	12.7	83.1	53.5	5.-	2.4	48.-
U.S.S.N.M. A.N.S.P.	1,732		—	—	18.4	13.7	14.1	74.5	76.6	102.9	87.9	15.40	—	6.9	14.2	—	48.6	5.2	2.4	46.2
	1,840		—	—	18.3	13.7	14.1	74.9	77.-	102.9	88.1	15.37	—	7.1	14.3	—	49.6	5.3	2.6	49.1
	15,490		—	—	18.-	13.8	14.6	75.6	81.1	107.4	92.4	15.60	—	7.2	13.5	—	53.3	5.1	2.75	53.9
	1,698		—	—	18.-	13.8	14.-	76.7	77.8	101.4	88.-	15.27	—	7.2	13.5	—	55.0	5.-	2.65	53.-
	1,105		—	—	17.6	13.5	13.7	76.7	77.8	101.5	88.1	14.93	—	n.6.7	13.4	—	56.9	5.4	2.5	46.3
	1,754		—	—	17.5	13.6	13.6	77.7	77.1	99.3	86.8	14.87	—	7.7	13.6	—	49.3	(cleft palate)		
	1,730		—	—	18.-	14.-	13.1	78.8	72.8	93.6	81.9	15.03	—	6.7	13.9	—	55.4	5.1	2.8	54.9
	1,708		—	—	18.-	14.-	13.6	76.4	76.4	97.1	85.5	15.13	—	7.7	12.9	—	51.0	5.1	2.65	52.-
	1,604		—	—	18.4	14.7	14.4	79.9	78.3	98.-	87.-	15.83	—	7.2	13.6	—	52.9	5.4	2.75	50.9
	1,707		—	—	17.9	14.5	13.9	81.-	77.6	95.9	85.8	15.43	—	7.1	13.4	—	53.-	5.2	2.7	51.9
MEANS, SEMINOLES					(11) 17.91	(11) 13.20	(11) 13.89	(11) 77.0	(11) 77.6	(11) 100.7	(11) 87.6	(11) 15.20		(11) 7.1	(11) 13.5	—	(11) 52.5	(10) 5.18	(10) 2.62	(10) 50.6

FLORIDA CRANIA (ALL)

FEMALES

Place:	No.	Locality	Deformation	Vault: Special	Vault: L.	B.	H.	C.I.	H.L.I.	H.B.I.	Mean H.I.	Cranial Module	Face: Ment.-Nas.	Alv.Pt.-Nas.	D.bizyg.max.	F.I. total	F.I. upper	Nose: L.	B.	N.I.
WEST COAST																				
U.S.N.M.	242,667	PENSACOLA BAY	mod. fr.-occ. flat.	—	(16.2)	(14.3)	(13.2)	—	—	—	—	—	11.6	7.-	12.8	90.6	54.7	—	—	—
	242,669	"	sl. occip. flat.	—	(16.-)	(14.4)	(14.-)	—	70.-	101.5	88.9	14.57	—	—	—	—	—	5.3	2.45	46.2
W. I.	15,857	HOPE MD., Anclote Key	—	—	17.2	13.4	13.6	77.9	—	—	—	14.80	—	—	—	—	—	5.2	2.5	48.2
U.S.N.M.	242,617	CEDAR KEYES	—	—	16.9	14.4	12.8	85.2	75.7	88.9	81.8	14.73	—	—	—	—	—	5.2	2.5	48.2
	242,694	"	—	—	17.-	14.1	—	82.0	—	—	—	—	—	—	—	—	—	—	—	—
W. I.	15,478	SAFFORD MD. Tarpon Springs	—	thick	17.2	14.6	—	84.9	—	—	—	14.70	—	7.4	—	—	—	—	—	—
	15,480	"	—	—	17.6	14.6	13.6	83.-	77.3	93.2	84.5	15.27	—	—	—	—	—	5.3	2.2	41.5
	15,483	"	—	—	17.6	14.-	—	79.6	—	—	—	—	—	—	—	—	—	—	—	—
	154,794	"	—	—	16.5	14.1	—	85.4	—	—	—	—	—	—	—	—	—	—	—	—
	154,839	"	—	—	17.2	13.4	12.6	77.9	73.3	94.-	82.4	14.40	—	7.3	—	—	—	5.2	2.3	44.2
	154,840	"	—	sl.	16.8	14.1	—	83.9	—	—	—	—	—	—	13.9	—	—	—	—	—
	154,957	"	—	asym.	17.6	14.8	n. 13.6	84.1	—	—	—	—	—	—	—	—	—	—	—	—
	154,962	"	—	—	16.4	14.3	14.3	87.2	82.9	95.1	88.6	14.77	—	7.1	—	—	51.1	—	—	—
U.S.N.M.	16,009	CLEARWATER, TAMPA BAY	sl. fr.-occ. flat.	—	(16.9)	(15.4)	—	(91.1)	—	—	—	—	—	—	—	—	—	—	—	—
	16,010	"	—	—	15.8	12.9	12.7	81.6	80.4	98.4	88.5	13.80	10.8	6.8	—	—	—	4.7	2.4	51.1
	243,692	"	—	—	17.7	14.-	13.4	79.1	75.7	95.7	84.5	15.03	—	—	—	—	—	—	—	—
	243,648	"	—	—	17.6	13.5	13.3	75.6	78.4	103.8	89.3	14.57	—	—	—	—	—	—	—	—
	243,637	"	—	—	17.3	13.6	14.2	78.-	82.1	105.2	92.2	15.-	—	6.6	—	—	—	—	—	—
	243,679	"	—	—	17.4	13.6	—	78.2	—	—	—	—	—	—	—	—	—	—	—	—
	243,645	"	—	—	17.5	13.7	—	78.3	—	—	—	—	—	—	—	—	—	—	—	—
	243,614	"	—	—	18.1	13.8	—	79.-	—	—	—	—	—	—	—	—	—	—	—	—
	243,674	"	—	—	17.3	14.3	14.8	79.8	83.1	103.5	92.2	15.63	—	—	—	—	—	—	—	—
	243,636	"	—	—	17.8	13.9	13.3	80.3	78.2	95.7	86.1	14.73	—	—	—	—	—	5.4	2.6	48.9
	243,643	"	—	—	17.-	14.3	—	81.8	—	—	—	—	—	—	—	—	—	—	—	—
	243,672	"	—	—	17.4	14.2	14.4	82.2	83.7	101.4	91.7	15.27	—	—	—	—	—	—	—	—
	243,642	"	—	—	17.2	13.4	13.3	82.6	78.2	99.2	87.5	14.57	—	—	—	—	—	—	—	—
A. N. S. P.	2,213	JOHNS PASS, Tampa Bay	—	—	17.-	13.4	—	78.8	—	—	—	—	—	6.8	13.3	—	51.1	5.-	2.6	52.-
	2,210	"	—	—	17.1	14.3	12.8	79.5	74.8	94.1	83.3	14.50	11.-	6.8	13.6	80.9	50.-	4.6	2.2	47.8
	2,215	"	—	—	17.6	14.7	13.7	81.2	77.8	95.8	85.9	15.20	11.5	7.1	13.4	86.5	53.4	4.9	2.5	51.-
	2,218	CHARLOTTE BAY AND Ft. MYERS	—	—	16.5	13.4	13.8	80.1	83.6	93.9	85.5	15.-	—	6.9	13.4	—	51.5	4.9	2.4	49.-
	2,227	"	—	—	17.5	14.5	13.5	84.3	81.3	96.4	88.2	14.70	—	6.7	13.7	—	48.9	4.7	2.3	48.9
U.S.N.M.	292,755	"	—	—	17.8	13.4	—	76.6	—	—	—	—	—	—	—	—	—	5.1	2.15	42.2
	292,752	"	—	—	17.4	14.4	13.2	81.5	74.2	91.-	81.7	15.17	—	—	—	—	56.2	5.2	2.4	46.2
	300,117	"	—	—	17.5	14.4	13.8	84.7	81.2	95.8	87.0	15.07	—	—	—	—	—	—	—	—
	292,751	"	sl. occip. flat.	—	17.-	13.5	14.-	77.1	80.-	103.7	90.3	15.-	12.3	7.6	13.7	89.8	55.5	5.-	2.45	49.-
	227,842	"	—	—	18.-	14.6	14.-	81.1	77.8	95.9	90.-	15.53	11.4	7.3	13.-	87.7	—	5.-	2.45	49.-
MEANS, WEST COAST:					(33) 17.23	(33) 14.-	(21) 13.56	(33) 81.2	(21) 77.4	(21) 97.2	(21) 86.2	(21) 15.02	(6) 11.4	(13) 7.-	(9) 13.4	(5) 87.-	(9) 52.4	(15) 5.05	(15) 2.4	(15) 47.5

Place	No.	Locality	Deformation	Vault:									Face:					Nose:		
				Special	L.	B.	H.	C.I.	H.L.I.	H.L.B.I.	Mean H.I.	Cranial Module	Ment.-Nas.	Alv. Pt.-Nas.	D. bizyg. max.	F.I. total	F.I. upper	L.	B.	N.I.
ST. JOHNS RIVER A.N.S.P.		ST. JOHNS RIVER																		
	1,794	Tick Id.	—	—	17.7	14.-	12.9	70.1	72.9	92.1	81.4	14.87								
	1,808	Huntoon Id.	—	—	17.5	13.9	14.-	79.4	80.-	100.7	89.2	15.13								
	1,787	Lake Co.	sl. front. flat.	—	n.17.1	14.3	—	81.9	—	—	—	—								
	1,795	Nowak Ldg.	—	—	17.2	14.3	14.-	83.1	81.4	97.9	88.9	15.17		6.4	12.8		50.-	4.9	2.-	40.8
	1,783	Tar Ldg.	—	—	15.9	13.6	13.8	85.5	86.8	101.5	93.6	14.43								
	1,789	Kitchen Creek	—	—	16.5	14.3	13.1	86.7	79.4	91.6	85.1	14.63								
	1,790	Mulberry Md.	—	—	16.7	14.7		88.-													
		MEANS, ST. JOHNS RIVER:			(7) 16.94	(7) 14.11	(5) 13.56	(7) 83.3	(5) 80.-	(5) 96.7	(5) 87.5	(5) 14.85								
EAST COAST U.S.N.M.	242,666	ST. AUGUSTINE			16.8	13.2	13.6	78.6	81.-	103.-	90.7	14.53		6.8	13.2	90.9	56.8	4.9	2.4	44.4
	242,685	"			17.-	13.9	—	81.8	—	—	—	—	12.-	7.5				5.4		
	242,686	"			16.8	13.9	13.3	82.7	79.2	95.7	86.6	14.67						4.9		
	242,627	NEW SMYRNA			17.4	13.3	14.-	76.4	80.5	105.3	91.2	14.90			h. 12.9					
	242,626	"			17.-	13.9	13.4	81.8	78.8	96.4	86.7	14.77								
	242,623	"			17.-	14.1	13.8	82.9	81.2	97.9	88.7	11.97								
	242,628	"			16.8	14.-		83.3													
		MEANS, EAST COAST:			(7) 16.97	(7) 13.75	(5) 13.62	(7) 81.1	(5) 80.1	(5) 99.6	(5) 88.8	(5) 14.78		(2) 7.15	(2) 13.05			(3) 5.1		
SOUTH AND SOUTHEAST FLORIDA U.S.N.M.		SOUTH AND SOUTHEAST FLORIDA:																		
	228,452	LAKE OKEECHOBEE	—	—	17.3	13.6	14.-	78.6	80.9	102.0	90.6	14.97						4.9		
	228,336	"	—	—	16.2	13.-	13.1	80.2	80.9	100.8	89.7	14.10		6.3				4.7		
	228,337	"			(15.2)	(12.6)	(12.8)	82.9	84.2	101.6	92.1	13.53								
		MEANS, SOUTH AND SOUTHEAST FLORIDA:			(3) 16.23	(3) 13.06	(3) 13.30	(3) 80.5	(3) 81.9	(3) 101.8	(3) 92.8	(3) 14.20								
SEMINOLES A.N.S.P.		SEMINOLE INDIANS																		
	1,788	VARIOUS	—	—	16.8	13.4	13.7	79.8	81.6	102.2	90.7	14.63		6.4	12.6		50.8	4.5	2.45	54.4
	1,726	"	—	—	16.6	14.1	13.4	84.9	80.7	95.-	87.3	14.70								
		MEANS:			(2) 16.70	(2) 13.75	(2) 13.55	(2) 82.3	(2) 81.2	(2) 98.6	(2) 89.-	(2) 14.67								
	729	SEMINOLE ADOLESCENTS	—	—	16.3	12.4	12.1	76.1	74.2	97.6	84.3	13.60								
	727	"	—	—	15.6	12.5	12.4	80.1	79.5	99.2	88.2	13.50								
		MEANS:			—	—		(4) 80.15	(4) 79.-	(4) 98.5	(4) 87.6	—								

INDEX

A

B

C

T

U

W

Y

Printed in the United States
70696LV00001B/4-102

9 780817 353599